REACHING

A Memoir

Grace Peterson

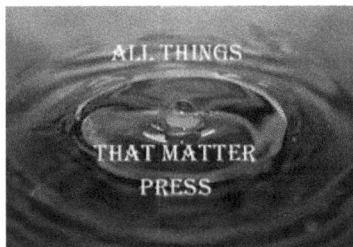

ALL THINGS

THAT MATTER
PRESS

ISBN: 978-0-9894032-0-7

Library of Congress Control Number: 2013939462

Cover Photo by Tracy Corey, tracyecorey@gmail.com

Cover by All Things That Matter Press

Published in 2013 by All Things That Matter Press

Acknowledgments

Thank you to Phil and Deb Harris of All Things That Matter Press for seeing merit in my work and guiding me to publication. It's an honor to work with you.

Thank you to Dr. Timothy McCarley, for fine-tuning my meds and to Dr. Stephen Brennan for your countless hours of listening and for helping me to identify and eventually shut off those old tapes. I was lucky to find you.

Thank you to Carol, Annie, Lynda, Cate, Connie and the rest of the GR Ladies for your unflinching smiles, your warmth and support; Sandra and Heather for your encouragement. Girlfriends rock.

Thank you to my many precious online friends for your generous camaraderie. You feed my soul.

Thank you to Laura for waiting and then forgiving me without hesitation. You're the best sister a person could ask for.

And finally, thank you to Steve for showing me unconditional love and to Dan, Mindy, Beth, Susan, for living your dad's example. You're the reason I'm still here. I love you.

For Valerie

AUTHOR'S NOTE

Authenticity is extremely important to me. My story is as true as my ability to remember it, without fabrications. My early years will feel somewhat random and disjointed as I put more effort into describing my surroundings than my feelings. This is how my memory works. Whether this is a natural part of brain development or my signature coping skill, in this book, I've sought to remain true to it.

Although my preeminent reason for writing this book is to reveal spiritual abuse, I write about my early years for two other reasons: first, to help the reader understand how my twisted family dynamic caused serious psychological damage that led to an ignorant worldview; second, to explore how that worldview led to a series of erroneous choices that caused further damage. In other words, I didn't just wake up one day and decide to identify myself as one of Brock's followers; there were three decades of history that led up to it.

I've taken *slight* liberties with time lapses between some events and verbatim dialogue. All names have been changed except Steve's.

There is no greater agony than bearing an untold story inside you.
~Dr. Maya Angelou

~ ~ ~

A writer must be true to himself, and let the chips fall where they may.
~John F. Kennedy

~ ~ ~

Maybe we were created yesterday with a memory to go with it.
~A Science Teacher

PROLOGUE

I'm savoring my final minutes of somnolence. Lying here, oblivion slightly out of reach, the baby sleeps and Steve snores intermittently. I don't have time to ascertain if the distant rumble is imagined or real because in a nanosecond deafening pandemonium has completely seized the terrain and everything seated upon it. *It's real.* The house rattles violently then coalesces with the rumbling of earth's underbelly as the geographic ogre rolls over, pulls the covers up, and goes back to sleep.

"Earthquake." I don't shout it. I state it like it happens every day, and right then I realize that in the back of my mind it *does* happen every day. It's happened every day since sixth grade in Hawaii when my classmates and I hid under our desks. But I've refused to acknowledge it until this moment when it's happening in the *front* of my mind.

I've sprung out of bed and floated to the dining room. The hanging lamp, oscillating violently above the table, is now the only indication that anything out of the ordinary happened. I breathe and turn my dizzy, disoriented self around, scanning the room.

Holy shit. The baby! When I ran out of the bedroom I left my helpless infant in the crib. What kind of a mother am I?

Steve and the three older children are a little shaken up but okay. The baby slept through it. She's okay.

They're fine. Everything's fine. We can all relax.

But I *can't* relax. I'm far from fine.

Everything is still foggy and in slow motion. I feel fifty pounds heavier and it's with great effort that I gather my wits and attempt to mother my children. I'm unable to form the words *don't leave* as I watch Steve close the door and head for work.

Like a turtle without a shell, I'm naked with nowhere to hide, no anchor. The defenses, the resting places, the link to reality, gone. My mind was messed up before, but now I feel as though I've completely lost it. I can't get warm and I can't find any comfort and I can't stop thinking that something terrible is going to happen at any second.

Anticipating doom requires enormous amounts of energy. Sleep is my only escape. I'm tired but I'm too scared to sleep.

There is no denying it. I've got to get help.

CHAPTER ONE

Her thin legs are crossed and pedal pushers expose her freckled calves. Despite a morning of relentless housekeeping, her red hair is perfectly coiffed save for one lock that intermittently disrupts her fixation with the *Reader's Digest* in her lap. Beside her, the blue ribbon launches upward until it hovers in a mist like an apparition looking down at the world it dominates.

I've tiptoed down the hallway and around the corner and, as I see her there, I finely tune my best lying voice. "I slept. I'm ready to get up now."

"March right back in there and go to sleep. Get a move on." And she's not kidding, either.

I tromp back to my bunk bed, defeated and a little scared. My ever-accessible thumb provides the comfort I seem unable to acquire from the adult world.

Vestiges of last night's potty tickle my nose as I strain to comprehend the mother's world so out of reach.

Sometimes her undertakings are obvious. The clicking of the adding machine means she's at the table. "Don't touch it," she'll warn, followed by, "I've got eyes in the back of my head." But all I see is her pretty red hair.

My restless body tosses and turns until I'm on my back looking up at the pillows protruding through the wire mesh holding Sarah's sagging top-bunk mattress. Her shrill "Mom" reminds me that she hates me poking her, even though I wasn't poking *her*.

The father's slide show is one of the few pleasant departures from his typically menacing nature. Banned from entry, his setup routine goes unseen until everything is to his satisfaction. As we find our places, there's a hum and a funny smell and a beam of light that catches millions of dust particles that look like tiny bugs dancing by moonlight. The beam lands on the screen, forming a perfectly white square. Then, with a methodic click and swish, a larger-than-life depiction of child-play swallows the square. My sisters and I love seeing ourselves on the screen.

The mother sits silently bottle feeding Adam. It's too dark to see the blue ribbon but the orange tip lights up when it gets close to her face.

I'm careful to interpret the mother's demeanor. She seems friendly, so I ask her about Adam and how he got here. And then I ask her how *I* got here.

The mother brusquely delivers the facts like they're hers but they're not. They're my mine and I hold tightly to them.

"Six-oh-six p.m., seven pounds, seven ounces, stormy night, and *you were all black and blue,*" she says, puffing on her cigarette, unconcerned with my fascination. I think about my little self and what bruises look like and feel a sense of triumph.

***

The familiar troll of the town's ice cream truck sashays on the summer breeze right through the screened door and into the front room. Adam is already asleep but Nellie, Sarah, and I are out the door and running to the top of Hollis Street where the truck has chugged to a stop and neighbors have lined up. I check and, yes, the dime is still squeezed into my sweaty palm.

As I dive into the curlicue, Nellie, who is much older says, "Hurry and eat it before it melts."

Eat it fast, before it melts is an unquestioned mantra that buffers the thrill of my very own ice cream cone and triggers a mysterious foreboding associated, I assume, with the mess of it all. Eat it fast because having it drip off the cone is the worst thing that could ever possibly happen.

Like the wild crayon-scribble that exemplifies my childish impetuosity, the last of the sun's rays light up crimson and orange in the western sky. The sisters are too busy eating it fast before it melts to detect my furtive assessment of things here at the top of Hollis Street. Donnie lives here.

***

I walk with him up Hollis Street to his house. He tells me playing in his father's shed will be fun.

There is very little space between the lawn mower and the many unidentifiables. He closes the door and slivers of daylight stream through screened openings by the roof. He likes me to pull down my pants. He likes me to lie down so he can lie down on me. I want to say no but *the bad* and *the no* are all mixed up.

Donnie invites me again and I hesitate, hoping this time we'll play something different. But it's always the same and eventually his pattern becomes something I can anticipate beforehand. The aversion to my own shame fuels my power to say no. And I learn that Donnie must be avoided at all cost.

As I carry my shame down Hollis Street, the western sky has morphed into an ominous dark hood and the wind is the scythe. I make a mad dash for the door, unable to silence the hypnotic dirge of the times.

*Let me tell you 'bout the birds and the
bees and the flowers and the trees
and the moon up above...*

CHAPTER TWO

The nice grandma wipes her hands on her apron as she emerges from the house, tottering precariously due to some inexplicable injury. She offers a tentative greeting and hands out cookies. The grandpa, with his Santa-like girth and demeanor, seems genuine and jovial as he wipes his blackened hands on a blackened cloth and lets out a windy cough.

Our extended family consists of two sets of grandparents—the nice grandma and grandpa and the mean grandpa and grandpa—and the scary aunt and the scary uncle. The mother and father like to let these relatives babysit us, but we only like coming here to the nice grandma and grandpa's house.

Adam is still too young, but Nellie, Sarah, and I are given free rein of the grandparents' expansive grounds. The river with its continual murmur is beyond an oval lawn and a slight drop-off. Thousands of oak trees umbrella the noonday sun, except in the garden where raspberries ripen and mahogany Black Eyed Susans bloom in a massive clump.

I'm one of the pretty ladies on TV, promenading down the grandpa's crunchy curving pathway singing "Would you like to ride in my beautiful balloon" to the audience seated in my imagination.

Breathing is much easier here where there is an easing of the rigorous rule-keeping and manners manifesto routinely enforced at home. While Nellie and the grandma work on enchiladas, Sarah, Adam, and I listen to the grandpa's stories. The bitter taste of his vino shivers in my mouth and I keep a tight hold on the special tiny glass that nearly duplicates the grandpa's bigger version. Dinner is also more tolerable thanks to pleasant talk and pleasant food. Even the grandma's salad is tasty enough to actually eat, devoid of that slimy mayonnaise and chunky blue cheese that habitually smothers the mother's rendition.

***

Hysterical tears and unabashed vocals mix with snot and errant tufts of hair in an effort to alert the mother of my displeasure. But I'm either ignored or misinterpreted because the paramount reasons for my protests, loud enough to rattle walls, refuse to permeate the mother's heart.

I'm placed inside the car, sardined between Nellie, Sarah, and the cousins, and we're pulling out of the driveway, onto Hollis Street, all the way to the scary aunt and scary uncle's house.

Their austere home is a testament to their demeanor, ironically only a few miles from the nice grandma and grandpa's equally telltale landscape. The scary uncle's rusty machinery hides unsuccessfully behind the garage. The scary aunt's clothesline, stationed in the center of dandelion-infested sprawl, lauds pant legs and pillowcases that covertly cavort in the scant breeze, the only movement other than an occasional tail flitting flies on the horses grazing in the adjacent pasture.

I'm too scared to say no when I'm lured into dark corners by Cousin Norbert. He's taken control, pulling down my pants and touching me, wanting me to touch him and our parts to touch. Escape is impossible, so I don't even think about forgetting it. I just forget it.

More disconcerting than Norbert's entanglements are those of his father, the scary uncle. While he's away, my personal rules for safety are fairly straightforward. Avoid alone time with Norbert.

With the scary uncle's return, my anxiety climbs, quickening my escape alarm. The outer extremities of the property are the safest and best vantage point for daydreaming and flying in my beautiful balloon all the way to the nice grandma and grandpa's home, just over the hill in the distance.

"Dinnertime! Come in and wash up," is followed by the scary aunt's individual summons, like we didn't hear her the first time. The mother does this, too, and it's the only time her voice sounds even remotely like I'm wanted or cared about.

Decades later, it is cause for speculation.

Maybe these 1960s housewives think that gathering their charges around their slaved-over meal will somehow erase all of the hurts and misunderstandings and keep the illusion of a happy family alive, the gold standard: perfect husband, perfect kids. But in my world, meal time just exposes and magnifies and irritates and exacerbates the whole nightmarish illusion; all these wills gathered around the table while the ringleader keeps vigil, poised for combat, alert for errancy, lording domination, coddling it, stroking it like a prized race horse, a gamble that pays off every time an order is flawlessly carried out, without any backtalk, raising well-behaved kids, good kids. Time bomb kids.

Entering the back door, I can hear the scary uncle barking his compulsory, "Wash up," in a voice far too loud to be friendly.

The sisters, Adam, and the cousins crowd around the tiny bathroom sink and fight over the single, inadequate stream of water splashing against a bevy of soiled hands and the dirty sliver of aromatic Dial soap on the verge of annihilation.

I hear the scary uncle utter something about hands and *face,* but I'm ignoring that. It's stupid. My face isn't dirty and besides, the father—who is *way* meaner than the scary uncle—doesn't require this so I must have heard wrong.

We file out of the bathroom toward the tiny kitchen booth and the scary uncle just watches with his signature countenance: half smile, half rage.

With steely eyes and pinched lips, he takes his work-worn hands and grabs and squeezes and turns child-sized hands over, checking both sides for some aberrant dirt spot because without its discovery and elimination, the world might end. Then he spends a few seconds sizing up the rest of the kid to see if she's passed muster.

And then he lords it over her for a few seconds, deciding whether this bratty little kid is worthy and deserving of this nice meal the scary aunt prepared.

Everyone else has passed and they sit.

The scary uncle looks at me with those eyes of steel. "Do you think you don't need to wash your face?" he snarls.

I look at him briefly then look down. Eye contact is impossible; I'm sure he's laboring to quell his impulse to annihilate me.

A manic parade of words stumble over themselves. How at *this* house we do what we're told and we don't come to dinner without washing our hands *and face* and if I want eat dinner here, I'll have to learn how to follow his rules, like being here is a privilege.

Turning on the water, unfortunately, fails to drown out the sound of clanking dishes in the other room. Twirling the dirty sliver of Dial, I hunch over the sink and force my hands to massage my face while the sink's black escape route has me mesmerized, wishing I could float on the water like the soapy bubbles and disappear into oblivion.

Escape is impossible, however, and now I must gather my wits, swallow my pride, ignore my humiliation, and wander out of this bathroom where inevitably all eyes will scan me and the scary uncle will, once again, size me up with his half smile/half rage glare and decide my fate. And then I'll be sentenced to a meal I have no desire to eat because my appetite, a few minutes ago a raging monster, has up and left.

CHAPTER THREE

The father's arm is draped over the front seat and his hand dangles beneath the mother's red hair. On his fingers are black hairs protruding intermittently between the tattooed letters spelling his name. As he drives, I'm lulled by the predictable kerthunk of undulating windshield wipers. We're on our way to our new house at Echo Bend.

Breaking my mental reverie, the father blasts Nellie, Sarah, and me with his latest imperative: "When we go inside, don't touch the walls." Then, without allowing time for digestion, he appends his decree with something about fresh paint and dirty hands, as he squashes any remaining excitement over seeing our new house.

From the massive living room window, I can see the North Umpqua River. It flows past our property at the bottom of the hill and, like most water courses, it alters its flow, color, and overall demeanor in reaction to the fickle skies. During the winter months it becomes a foreboding muddy torrent, swelling well beyond its borders, submerging the stones and grasses; sometimes you can even see a log carried downstream in a frantic bounce. But in summer, the river has resumed its gentle cadence. This is the river that drew the father here. On weekends, he'll grab his fishing gear and head down to catch a steelhead.

I'm also drawn to the river. I like spending my days on its shore, immersed in the scent of exposed algae cooking in summer's heat and watching slender blades of grass dance to the water's rhythm.

On those days when I foolishly venture too close to the father, he plays the toss-me-into-the-water game. Ignoring my ear-splitting protestations, I'm heaved into icy liquid. After sinking for a few seconds, my body rises just enough to cough and gasp for air as my appendages involuntarily flail and splash more water onto my face and into my eyes. Down again and my nostrils, eyes, and throat sting while my panicked screaming coalesces with the sound of submerged bubbles. I rise again, just long enough to realize I'm drowning. The river is swallowing me, winning the battle to rid me of my existence. And why shouldn't it? It's bigger and stronger than me. I'm just a stupid, helpless little girl who got too close to the father.

Somehow I make it to the shallow places, but how I get here, I'm not sure. I climb out, slowed by the weight of the orange lifejacket straddling my shoulders. The father must not have known what he was doing. He didn't mean to drown me—or did he?

But then, he'll do it again and again and finally it will make sense. The father wants to drown me. So I will keep my distance from him out here by the river.

At eight years old, my primary function is self-preservation, and I'm finding that the father doesn't need to be nearby to feed my growing anxiety with life. By proxy it's taken on a life of its own and, despite its unpleasantness, I welcome it. The mishaps and subsequent lessons learned feed this strange father-like guardian and it grows while I search for adult-free activity.

In part, it must be my predisposition. Unlike the rest of the family, I'm hyper, impetuous. I embark without thinking, which puts me at greater risk for injury and increases my demand for this guardian.

For instance, twirling around the expansive living room, I'm jarred into reality following a mysterious onslaught of searing pain in my big toe. The mother, exasperated, pulls the errant sewing needle, then dismisses me.

"It won't stop hurting, Mom." I'm back and pleading, begging the mother to right this seriously painful wrong.

"I pulled out the needle. It shouldn't be hurting anymore." Maybe it shouldn't, but it does. Something's wrong with me.

Like the shrill of an alarm clock, toe pain obliterates my ability to sleep. By morning, the pain hasn't eased at all. As I'm drawn to its source, I can see what appears to be the tip of the sewing needle breaking through the swollen, red skin near my toenail. I wake Nellie to inform her that I've found a secret weapon just like on *Get Smart*. Should someone step on my toe, they'll get poked!

"Mom, Dad, you need to see this," Nellie says.

During those brief interludes when my need for oxygen briefly silences my hysterics, I can hear the father calling me in the tone I dread.

"Hold still, dammit," He grabs one of his medical tools and extracts the remaining needle.

***

Just past the nearest upstream neighbors, the next mishap occurs. A rocky precipice juts out, exposing a geologist's dream. There is a narrow trail embedded in the rock that wends its way to the top of the ridge. A clump of effusive, orange California poppies catches my eye and adds to the allure.

I inch my way upward while tightly grasping any available rocks and grasses. At the top, with just enough room to sit, I drink in my heightened vantage point. I'm level with the oak treetops; the river plays peek-a-boo through their verdant branches. I allow the velvety thin poppy petals to caress my nose, breathe in their piquancy, and catapult this moment into the realm of lifetime achievement.

I'm feeling rather smug with my abilities so, as I make my descent, I declare it fitting to reward myself with a handful of plump blackberries growing in an enormous mound near the bottom of the cliff.

Perhaps it's my childish zeal or primal hunger that has blinded me to the voluminous gray cone hidden deep within the briars. Its inhabitants have better eyesight and hone mine as a legion of protectors swarms in my direction.

Errant grass blades swoosh past my face in my attempt to outrun the air patrol dispatched to annihilate me. My caterwaul could break glass and, from the corner of my eye, a woman on the opposite side of the river stands on her deck and looks in all directions. I know she's looking for me, but she can't see me—because I don't want her to.

Eventually the bees retreat and I can catch my breath. In serious pain, I make my way home to indifferent parents.

I'm tired, lying on my bed, surveying hundreds of swollen red spots scattered over my legs and arms like splashed paint. Poppies, blackberries, and treetops keep trouncing through my brain like a happy parade of accomplishments. At the end of the parade, a swarm of bees chases me home.

***

Financial obligations must be a stretch for the parents because now the mother is working during the day. Sadly, little Adam isn't here, either. I miss my little brother. I can't understand the deep, painful emotions I have for him and the powerlessness I feel over his absence.

After school, I'm indoors by the living room windows creating a world for Adam's cars and trucks. Roads intersect through the 1960s blue and green shag carpet. I'm the bus driver taking kids home from school. It is routine play until my silence is usurped by a rumble, a pulse, and an earsplitting rattle. Sarah runs out from the bedroom. "What was that?"

"I don't know, but the windows were all rattling." I reply, standing now, anticipating more.

But there is no more. Just the one event and it remains a mystery until the mother informs Sarah and me that a large truck driving along the highway miles away caught on fire. What we heard was the cargo of explosives that ignited and blew up.

On a subsequent trip to town, the mother points out the area of blackened earth. Perhaps a lingering look and detailed explanation would sate my cerebral cause and effect needing to steady itself, but the mother drives on.

***

Tensions at home seem to be on the rise. Especially at meal time while we're all forced into one room.

"Lean up," the father bellows, presumably to rectify the childish disarray surrounding him, as we did have a tendency to slouch back, rather than sit all prim and proper.

Perhaps in weaker moments he's aware of the tension he causes and uses his wry laughter to lighten the mood. But when accompanied by his latest taunt, the demanded response is merely compliance to garner approval.

"Garbage gut," he'll sneer at Sarah, sporting the marks of the most adept sociopath.

"Don't leave the vacuum cleaner in one place while it's running or it will burn the carpet," he shouts above the drone. The haunting image of the charred earth beside the highway is my further reinforcement.

"Don't touch the walls. Turn off the lights," he hollers.

***

Admittedly, I harbor a morbid fascination with the parental acrimony gaining momentum around me. Embedded in my psyche is this intangible need to know, to somehow make sense of my mixed up world. What are they fighting about?

So, on the periphery, my own internal battle ensues. In one corner, the peace-seeking part entices me to run, get outside where it's safer and let the chips fall where they may. In the other corner is the storm-chaser part who feels the need to dive right into the middle of things and form some kind of understanding about it all, and maybe even avert any more damage, if possible.

The mother and father are in their bedroom. The door, although closed, is incapable of buffering the role reversal: the mother yelling at the father.

"Don't go down there," Nellie warns.

Her bossiness just fuels my defiance as I stomp down the hall, uttering "I've had just about enough of this."

I burst open the door.

Before I can speak, the mother screams, "Get out." At least I think it's the mother. Or maybe a monster from *Dark Shadows*.

She walks toward me and, as I step back, she slams the door and resumes her tirade.

As I totter back down the hall toward Nellie, she whispers, "They're getting a divorce."

CHAPTER FOUR

The trees and grasses and fences and barns are the same ones I see while bouncing along in the school bus. For three years now North Bank Road has been a part of my daily regimen, familiar and comforting. But normal just exploded and the familiar is gone, replaced with the blackened void.

As the mother skillfully advances or retreats, depending on how one looks at it, I sit silently in the car and wonder if I'm leaving our home by the river for the last time.

A curve and a dip and as I look out, I see a thickening of trees. They cast an eerie darkness inside the mother's car. It seems fitting for my mood. As I mentally replay the events, a voice from somewhere whispers, *this is all a dream. Pretend it's all a dream.* I'm dreaming all of this and I'll wake up when it's over.

Hints of black pepper and stale cigarette smoke linger at the mean grandma and grandpa's small town house, hovering like a lifeless fog. The aging, plastic window coverings withhold daylight and fresh air like they're things accursed. They crinkle and eventually tear apart when I try unsuccessfully to raise them and I'm sure the mean grandma will not be happy when she sees what I've done. But she is in Hawaii with the mean grandpa right now so I won't worry about it.

The bathroom is stationed between two bedrooms. The grandpa must have forgotten to take his razor to Hawaii. This is good news for me since I'm here alone and I've always wanted to get a closer look at it and maybe even try it out on my face exactly how the mean grandpa does. Following a bit of contemplation, I choose a side, bring it to my face and begin to shave, mentally chanting, don't cut yourself, don't cut yourself.

Within seconds, I cut myself. A sharp sting is followed by an emerging red line right above my lip that grows fatter and begins to drip into the pristine sink below. It's a potent cause and effect, worthy of intensive study as I drop the razor, grab a Kleenex and press it against the wound to stop the blood flow that is now beginning to worry me.

***

As fellow classmates parade past me toward the swings and monkey bars, I reacquaint myself with the daunting openness of the playground. Although I was a first grader here before the move to the house by the river, I'm clearly an outsider now. I feel very alone and everything is alien including this strange series of emotions that are washing over me. With the parents' divorce and the move, I had been riding the current, holding on to myself while the familial storm raged around me. But here with all of these schoolmates my grip has turned to mush.

The overwhelming, crushing feeling of aloneness is followed by a moment of clarity as the mother's "quit feeling sorry for yourself" mantra streams through my mind. Not here. You can't cry here.

In addition to keeping my eyes dry, seeing Donnie is my biggest worry here at school. Although I try to shove his memory out of my consciousness, it lingers and haunts me, punishes me with missives of shame and disgust. Despite my protest, my mind harkens back to how he was able to lure me into his father's shed and how I was unable to say no to the things he told me to do. I'm terrified of seeing Donnie. However, I've relaxed a little since discovering that he's situated in the other third grade classroom. So far, I've been able to avoid him.

"Grab your chair and stand by the door," Mrs. Smith says.

I comply, since drawing attention to myself would make it a hundred times worse. Panic pulses through my veins and I don't possess the wherewithal or maturity to rationalize or pep talk myself out of it. I'm going to the other third grade classroom, the room where Donnie is.

On the big screen, Santa's antics fail to comfort me. Fortunately, Donnie is seated across the room, but even with him at that distance I can't concentrate on anything. I want to go home, escape this manufactured nightmare.

Several deep breaths and the comfort of dark, crowded seclusion begins to loosen the noose. I'm comforted by the sound of Santa's laugh and his rosy cheeks and bulging bag of wrapped presents. I asked the mother for a dollhouse and so I'll think about this instead of Donnie.

The school bus drops me off a few blocks from the mean grandma and grandpa's house. With the mother working and Adam at the babysitter's, I have the solitary freedom I've come to relish. After foraging for a snack I sit on the sofa and listen to the familiar sounds of *Perry Mason* and *The Big Valley*.

The garage is completely devoid of contents save for one box sequestered high on what might be an unreachable shelf. It's got me curious.

"I wonder why they didn't take that box to Hawaii with them," I comment to Sarah when she gets home from school. "What's in there?"

"Let's find out," is the reply I was hoping for.

With no ladder in sight, the empty shelves become ladder rungs and, miraculously, without any mishaps, the box is on the floor.

I grab the top magazine and thumb through the pages. Sarah grabs the second. Picture after close-up picture of women posing with no clothes on, their legs pulled apart, exposing hairy and pink secret places, resting on satin, accompanied by bejeweled hands, nippled ivory breasts, make-up and beauty marks and starched hair.

"I don't want to see anymore," I tell Sarah.

"Me, neither."

Climbing and carefully balancing ourselves, we're able to heave the box back to its original place.

Sarah whispers, "They must be Grandpa's."

I nod and don't think about it anymore because it's weird.

***

Nellie is living with the father. We haven't seen her since fleeing the house by the river and I doubt we'll see her this Christmas. It was a year ago when she skillfully convinced me that Santa Claus was just pretend but until now, as I glide through store aisles, with familiar Christmas tunes emanating from somewhere, it has never occurred to me that someone actually has to buy the presents and the wrapper and ribbons. Here it all is in plain view, ready to purchase. How strange. How exhilarating.

It's still dark as we amble into the mean grandma's bedroom where the mother sleeps.

"We're ready to open presents!"

The mother turns on the tree lights and sits in the chair with her thin legs curled up under her bathrobe. With disheveled hair and pale, pre-Revlon eyes and lips, this is an unfamiliar rendition of a pre-coiffed mother and makes me slightly ill at ease. Her fingers simultaneously cradle a coffee cup and lit cigarette with its blue ribbon rising undisturbed toward the ceiling.

Sarah and Adam are happily opening presents.

For reasons I can't assimilate, I seem to be somewhere else and an angry little ragamuffin has taken my place. Or maybe this is the real me and the happy girl was the imposter. Whatever the case, I'm irritated with everyone and everything. I can feel myself inching closer toward a full blown out-of-control rage and I wish everyone would quit making me mad.

I've become the father.

I want to hit and scratch and scream at everybody because something inside me is hitting and scratching and screaming to get out.

The dollhouse is not assembled. It's just a bunch of flat metal sheets intended to serve as walls, stamped with dollhouse décor. Sitting horizontal in its box, it fuels my smoldering rage.

"Stu will put it together tonight," the mother promises, trying to salvage a modicum of Christmas joy and assure me that her new boyfriend is every bit as capable of these things as the father.

I'm too angry to enjoy Christmas this year. Everything is wrong and everything makes me mad. Everything. Nothing is right and I can't make myself happy. No matter what I do, I can't be happy this Christmas.

We finish breakfast and the mother drives us to the scary aunt and the scary uncle's house. This could explain some of my misery but there is no talking to the mother about it. She is completely devoted to her brother and sister-in-law and expects us to enjoy going there.

***

I draw the drapes because it's getting dark and I like them covering the window at night. Sarah, Adam, and I have the TV on and jubilant voices are declaring that a new "decade" is imminent while, in the background, fancy people act happy, dancing to clarinet music.

The mother just left. She's going on a date with Stu. She doesn't mind leaving us home while she's gone. This is another adjustment in the multitude of adjustments I'm forced to absorb: the mother leaving us alone at night like this.

Sarah wants to stay up until midnight. Adam is too little and goes to bed. We watch TV, but my eyelids are heavy and 1970 has the audacity to roll in without my consent.

***

One of the mean grandma and grandpa's bookshelves holds a stack of brochures. Once more, I study the pictures of Hawaii and try to put a positive spin on the whole affair. Lots of green grass, palm trees, sandy beaches, and flowers, Hawaii will be a fun place, I tell myself.

Everything but the barest necessities is packed into a big box and the mother says she's having it shipped to Hawaii. Even the Christmas presents have gone missing. It's like saying goodbye and mourning my best friend, maybe worse. I really like my toys.

***

A glint of morning sunlight silhouettes the rolling hills far to the east. Goodbye, I whisper to my former existence and the fading memory of dwelling in the house by the river, back when my life was good.

Seated behind the scary uncle, the long drive up Interstate 5 to the airport allows me time to think. The mother tries to excite Sarah, Adam,

REACHING

and me about Hawaii, but I find it difficult to grasp. Everything is happening so fast there's little time for making sense of any of it.

Sitting motionless and white-knuckled, the movement of the airplane causes my every muscle to tense. I'm cemented in my own panic and the cabin's walls are closing in on me. I can't breathe. I'm sweating. We're not propelled along by engine thrust, we're floating and we're falling. I'm sure we're falling and we're going to die. My heart must be pushing upwards of a thousand beats per minute.

There is no escape, only the blue ocean, miles below.

"Are those clouds down there? Are we really that high up?" I ask Sarah, trying to calm myself with a distraction.

"I think so."

But this can't possibly be right. That puffy carpet of cotton balls so far down there can't possibly be the upside of the very clouds I see from the ground. If they are, this would confirm that we're riding extremely high in the sky. I refuse to believe Sarah's simple "I think so." She's wrong.

So without really thinking about it, I assign this new rule to my thinking. It goes something like if it's too unbelievable, it isn't true.

"I can't believe it so it's not true," I repeat to myself and I shake my head to an imaginary audience to reinforce my new resolve.

But maybe this is nothing new. Maybe I've been thinking this way all along and only now have I become aware of it.

We're total opposites, Sarah and I. She tries to get me to calm down and see things from a rational point of view but usually that just makes me angry and I lash out and we start fighting. It's hard to admit I'm wrong all the time.

The mother sits across the aisle, svelte, polished, elegant. Observing her there in that airplane seat, there's no denying her sophistication. Attractively poised, slim legs crossed, slender fingers hugging a cigarette with its elegant blue ribbon crashing against the airplane's ceiling, she absentmindedly clicks Wrigley's spearmint gum while absorbed in a book. Adam sits next to her, asleep. Both he and the mother are more like Sarah, calm, relaxed and sensible. Baffling.

For the duration of this flight to our new world called Hawaii, my eyes oscillate from the preoccupied mother, Adam, and Sarah on my left, to the window and the puffy mysterious things down below, back and forth, trying to make sense of this world and trying—fruitlessly—to relax.

CHAPTER FIVE

A breath of moist Tropicana envelopes me as I step off the airplane. Instinctively, I rub my hands and scan my surroundings. The airport's single story rooftop sits in the foreground while in the distance, buildings and trees vie for dominance. Above a wispy fog, golden afternoon sunlight announces that it's late afternoon.

The tarmac is mysteriously empty. I had hoped for a festive greeting with grass skirts and hula dance but reality has issued miles of inhospitable blacktop instead. Certainly the tradition of a smile and a lei around my neck would make me feel special in this special place. Like I *belonged*, like I was *welcome* here; like it was okay.

The familiar face of the mean grandma offers a mixture of comfort and dread. She offers her best "aloha" surrounded by a tight lipped smile that reads of a covert dissonance. And it warns me of its impending greeting later at home.

Amid adult chatter and controlled chuckling, I squeeze into the backseat of the grandma's Plymouth Fury, shipped here from the Oregon shores so far away.

Remembering the brochure pictures, I expect the landscape to consist of large sweeps of verdant lawn punctuated with palm trees and effulgent red florals, but this is not the case. Hawaii's landscape, once we're past the miles of sugarcane fields, seems more in keeping with southern Oregon's tawny grass, minus the rolling hills. The oak trees are replaced with intermittent mango groves and scrub *Ohia lehua* trees.

Eventually, we come to a large sign labeled "Hawaiian Paradise Park" yet I see no park and no paradise, just this salient contrivance protruding from the pervasive sea of grass and unidentifiable shrubbery. A little further and the grandma turns onto what I'll later identify as Makuu Drive. Descending numbers identify a series of gravel roads that intersect Makuu and form a large grid that spans several miles; a "subdivision," the mother says.

The mean grandma guides the Fury up a gentle incline, turns off 14th Avenue and pulls into the cemented carport. Stretching my legs, I notice a pervasive stillness that screams: this place is the quintessence of *remote*. A few rooftops dot the landscape miles away, but mostly it's just grass, shrubbery, and trees in every direction, save for the narrow band of blue to the east—the Pacific Ocean.

The grandma walks to the opposite side of the house and now I can hear what sounds like a very loud lawn mower.

"What is that?" I ask the mother.

"It's the generator," she says absentmindedly, dragging a suitcase toward the door. Later, Sarah tells me that because there is no electricity out here, the grandparents use this deafening machine to make electricity. This seems odd to me, being out here in the peace and quiet and yet never getting to hear it because that loud motor is going all the time.

The mean grandma doesn't like having us here. Her superficial pleasantries are code for "Be on your best behavior or else." She expects us to use our "manners." She won't tolerate silly noises or childish movement or any stuff lying around. Should I banish my manners and start acting like a kid, her tone will take on a decidedly glowering, irritability.

"Be still," she'll command. Or, "You mustn't swivel in the chair."

This is just how the grandmother is. I really don't want to be around her at all but I'm stuck here with her here the middle of nowhere, in the middle of the Pacific Ocean.

***

With post-dinner fatigue, we're all gathered around the tiny black and white. Rabbit ears veer precariously toward civilization while *Born Free* competes with the constant snowy interference. The roar of the generator fuels the TV, and, as I look at the imposing machine just outside the window, I make a mental note to keep away from it.

"That woman on TV doesn't look like the picture in the book," I venture.

The mother, on the verge of losing patience, explains that, "the woman on TV is an *actress*." Then adopting *her* mother's vernacular, "Now *be still* so we can hear it."

A notable pang of anxiety is no match for my curiosity. "What's an *actress*?" I blurt, looking straight at the mother. She doesn't answer because she's already answered a thousand questions and she's tired and clearly annoyed.

The *Born Free* anthem grabs my attention as the great lion Elsa reveals her cubs to the elated caretaker, Joy Adamson. Cavorting playfully, the cubs tug at my heart, causing an unavoidable river of tears to well up and flow down my cheeks.

"It's okay to cry," the grandma comforts, looking straight at my mortified face.

***

My breath is fogging the window as I labor to gain an image of the tiny town passing before me. Everything seems kind of dirty and dusty. The buildings hugging the main street are built of aged wood and conjoined by a central boardwalk for pedestrians. If the cars and electrical poles weren't here I'd expect Clint Eastwood to come riding through on his horse. We've already passed the only signs of Americana: a Dairy Queen and an American flag sitting flaccid atop its towering pole in front of a brand new United States Post Office.

The bus turns down a narrow road, then pulls up to a curb in front of the gym. Smaller buildings are scattered throughout the campus grounds, affecting a less imposing scene than the typical lone structure of mainland schools.

A group of dark-haired Hawaiian kids stands at the bottom of the stairs that lead up to what Sarah, Adam, and I will learn are the third through fifth grade classrooms. I try not to stare but it looks like they're just a bunch of squalid, younger boys. A few cover their bare feet with dusty thongs and the rest are barefoot. Each is proudly attached to a blue vinyl Pan Am book bag.

It appears they're mumbling something about us.

"Haole," one boy mutters.

"What are you doing at *our* school, haole?" another voice demands in a distinctly Hawaiian parlance that I've never heard before today.

"Go home, fuckin' haole," comes a third voice, fueled by the venom of his buddies and the sorry sight of three blonde-headed *freaks* invading their school.

I guess they want us to say something, respond to their peculiar directive, but I can't talk.

Not only can I not talk, I can't move. I'm stupefied.

Maybe this is just an anomaly, a few restless kids having a little fun. But maybe not. It dawns on me that there were a few covert mutterings on the bus, too. What does *haole* mean?

The attitude of my new classmates seems unanimous and unflinching. It quickly morphs into pervasive harassment that—for now—borders just this side of violence. Void of alternatives, and fearful of conflict, my mind scrambles for an escape route, a numbing routine, a way to cope with kids who hate me simply because my body's features are lighter in color. I can't do anything about my blonde hair or fair skin and I can't make myself invisible, so I just resign myself to the fact that these people hate me.

"Fuckin' haole. Why you come here? You fuckin' ugly, haole. Man, go home," they drone, one after the other, laughing at their ability to frighten me.

There's no safety. I'm perpetually on edge. Simple things such as walking to the bathroom incite a compulsion to look behind me, around me, check my surroundings and anticipate the impending threats and how I will escape them.

"Fuckin' haole bitch, this is *our* bathroom," the older girls yell. "Get the fuck out of here," they taunt while looking over the stall at my exposed shell.

I'm unable to think clearly. I rush to get away and learn to hold it. School becomes the most devastating place on the planet.

***

"Is our stuff here yet?"

"Not yet." The mother sounds like she's just as mad as I am about the lost stuff from the mainland, but then I think maybe she's just annoyed that I ask her the same thing every single night when she gets home.

Sarah, having heard this exchange, relieves the frustrated mother by reminding me for the hundredth time that the stuff isn't *lost*, it's still locked inside a *barge* and the workers are too busy *striking* to unload it. But this terse explanation doesn't comfort me. I've almost forgotten what I got for Christmas. I'm not a patient girl. This is just one injustice too many.

The mother, seated at the table, calms her nerves with a cigarette. Its blue line veers up and over her silky red hair in obedience to the gentle trade wind that wafts from the open window. She scans the pile of mail, silent. I see this as a posture fitting to voice my other major discontent.

"The kids at school don't like us, Mom. You said the Hawaiians were nice, but we just make them mad. They call us 'haole' and they call Sarah 'pollution' and sometimes we get in fights. The Hawaiian kids are mean and I don't like them."

The mother sighs, drops the mail on the table and smashes out her cigarette. She gets up and heads to the kitchen to make dinner. Maybe she'll talk to us at dinner. But she doesn't, and she never discusses it, because she doesn't like it when people complain.

***

School is a constant source of trauma, but once I'm home, I spend my time outdoors, exploring. Although I relish the alone time, it's not without its risks. I must keep on the alert here, too, because should I veer into the realm of disobedience, I will anger the ominous, unseen presence that watches me. It might be the volcano goddess *Pele*. She owns all the land and roams, watching for violators. When she finds the unfortunate souls, she'll spout lava on them. I can feel her watching me all the time when I'm outside.

I like to look for interesting things to plant in the lava-laden front yard. I've got a mysterious need to make the area pretty, so I look for plants to dig up and replant in the deep pockets of dirt amid the swirly *pahoehoe*, the mother calls it.

The mother is not a gardener, but she likes animals and brings home two cats.

Mickey disappears but Prissy becomes a mother.

We look in all the logical places but we can't figure out where she's hidden her children until we follow her up the road to a clump of greenery growing in the middle of the knee-high grass. There they are, huddled together in a pile.

"We can't leave them here. They'll get rained on."

Sarah runs home, gets a box, and the rescue operation is a success.

***

Thunder crackles, booms, and rattles the house like a million marching soldiers on the roof. I'm not fond of thunderstorms. On this night, what has become a pervasive anxiety is nearing the worst kind of panic.

My body feels detached, floating into the mother's bedroom and around the corner to her small bathroom. She stands fixated on her image in the mirror.

"Where are you going?" I ask in a futile appeal for motherly comfort.

"I'm going out." Her voice is neutral.

My world is dizzy, so to stay upright, I plaster my body against the bedroom wall at a predictably safe distance from the mother. Her Windsong perfume hits my nostrils and conveys her resolve. She'll be leaving in a few minutes. Ordinarily this wouldn't bother me. I've gotten used to her clandestine outings. But tonight is different. The storm's fury has transformed my typically independent self into a bundle of needy nerves.

A particularly earsplitting thunderbolt crashes into—or nearby—the house and my desperation forces anguished words out of my mouth.

"Can you stay home tonight? I'm scared. This storm is really bad, Mom. Please." I'm beyond reason, tears streaming down my face.

The mother is impervious to whining. It bothers her when I go on like this and my pleading has undoubtedly fueled an even stronger determination to leave. I know this and I should stop crying but I can't.

"Oh, for crying out loud." She finishes her primping ritual with a hissing aerosol application to her puffy hair, now dyed snow white.

"Don't leave, Mom. I'm scared. Please,"

The last rumble brought Sarah and Adam. They're quiet, but their faces reveal their fear.

Refusing to be manipulated, the mother utters her predicable, "Honestly, quit bawling," as she grabs her purse and heads for the door, leaving Sarah and Adam and me to ride out the storm alone, like Prissy's kittens huddled together in the grass.

With mystical force, a metaphysical energy, the repeated anguish has contorted and swelled and collapsed my psyche like a pliable ball of clay and shaped it into something familiar, a sort of pacifistic blob. With the fires of the storm, the clay has hardened around my gray matter. Inexplicable, it's a concession of sorts, a resolve, a numbing. Detachment.

I don't need her. I *won't* need her. I don't even want her to be my mother.

Without really thinking about it, at nine years old, I begin living my life as an orphan, a motherless daughter, emotionally independent.

CHAPTER SIX

The exact number of physical altercations eludes me but I can say with certainty that I am never the instigator. I hate conflict. No, the instigator is always some angry Hawaiian boy, apparently taught that it's okay to verbally disparage the dreaded *haole*. It's also fair game to pinch my boobs or my butt. From what I can tell, not only is it sanctioned, it's applauded.

I can take it for a while but, at some indefinable moment, I will snap and a seething rage will highjack my better thinking. Devoid of restraint, I grab the offender, throw him on the cement and beat him senseless. He fights back but all I can feel is blood surging through my veins, my flushed face, my inability to hear or see anything through the fog on the outside of my rage bubble.

Still, I don't fight as much as Adam does. Nearly every single day I hear that a teacher has to break up a fight involving him. This just kills me inside; the poor little brother I'm powerless to protect. I see the familiar sadness and abandonment in his eyes and, alarmingly, I see the familiar rage, too.

I tried, I think just one other time, after a particularly brutal day, to talk to the mother about my discontent with school. I imagine Sarah and Adam have made similar attempts. But complaints—undoubtedly in the form of childish whining—fall on the deafest of ears. The mother has made it plain that she doesn't like complainers. All I'll hear is her predictable, "Oh, quit feeling sorry for yourself," as she lights a cigarette that ostensibly signals my dismissal.

Although I've distanced myself from the mother, I'm still learning from her actions, echoing her behavior. She's made it abundantly clear that emotions are a nuisance, an irritant, a menace, a bother, a headache, something to be eliminated like garbage. So, by default, I follow her cue and apply it inward.

"Quit feeling sorry for yourself," I chide as I cut lines into my legs or arms because I have no tolerance for these dreadful feelings.

Not merely intolerant of my own feelings, I've amassed a pathological intolerance for Sarah's or Adam's feelings as well. Fist fights, hair pulling, biting, scratching, it's all a constant stream of power struggles, each of us is trying, unsuccessfully, to reconcile our own inner turmoil and powerlessness by dominating the weaker sibling, hoping this will make us feel alive inside.

Outside alone, riding my bike, looking for plant treasures, forging an independent, emancipated play world for myself, this is the only way I can experience anything even remotely pleasurable. But I'm always worried I'll do something stupid and anger the Hawaiian deities that hover with judgmental eyes and remind me that I'm trespassing and had better tread lightly.

***

A short gravel drive will bring the rare visitor to an open carport where the mother stations her "demo" Mazda. Behind it are two large storage closets with sliding doors painted dark brown. As long as the doors are closed, the mother's freezer is hidden. But sometimes we forget to close them when we leave. I worry that anybody could help themselves to the stuff inside.

I can just picture some unscrupulous stranger driving by. He sees that no one is home and waltzes right up the driveway, into the carport, right to that white freezer. And this is a violation I can't bear to think about, even though I do—all the time.

Maybe the mother doesn't care because we live in the country where people are few or maybe there is nothing in the freezer worth stealing. Still, every time I'm in the garage I slide the door closed and I always try to remember to close it before leaving for school. Hiding the freezer just makes me feel better.

Behind the freezer closet is the rainwater catchment tank. All the houses around here have them because the ground is too solid for well-drilling. Rainwater hits the roof then rolls downward to the gutters which carry it to this holding tank. A submerged pump brings it inside the house.

Sometimes we climb the ladder and peek into the tank to see how much water is there because during the dry season it can get pretty low. If it gets too low, a truck has to bring water to fill it and the mother says this is very expensive. Looking into the rectangular brick structure is a bit dizzying, especially when the water level is high and I can see through the wavy water to the depths below. The water is always dark and ugly. Later, I'll wonder how it is that none of us got extremely ill from drinking it.

***

"If you kids want to earn some money this summer, then pull all the weeds in the front yard," the mother suggests one early summer evening while the blue line dances with the trade winds.

I listen and watch her as she demarcates several areas of equal size—an odd thing indeed since she rarely ventures outside, except to climb into her car.

I've concluded that since the boring Watergate hearings are preempting my beloved "so poppers" I might as well earn some money. Perhaps this is the mother's idea, too.

"Each area that you clear of all weeds will earn you five dollars. When it's all done, I'll take you to Hilo," the mother promises.

I tackle three areas and earn myself a whopping fifteen dollars, an amazing amount of money for a twelve year old in 1973.

Sequestered in a miasma of blue smoke, the familiar landmarks whiz by but can't hold my interest. It's the ominous, charred and blackened turn in the road I'm looking for. I'm hoping that another sighting will explain the dark anxiety, the deep ache in my chest, the heavy sadness, the horror of death. Our friends, here one day and gone the next.

I picture their car tearing down the road way too fast. The essence of vulnerability huddles in the backseat. Maybe they're scared because their mom is acting *really, really* weird. Or maybe it's so late that they're sleeping. The car crosses the centerline, then the oncoming lane. It goes off the road and hits a rocky upraised area. The speed forces the car up the cliff several feet and then gravity forces it back to earth and it turns over, crashes down and bursts into flames.

This might not be how it happened but it's how I picture it happening when I look at that charred place on the side of the highway. It makes me sick. I don't know how else to deal with this whole mysterious thing called *death* so I play it over and over in my mind, trying to form it into something that makes sense.

I'm perplexed by the idea that friends can be living one day—you're playing with them and noticing everything about them like their pretty eyes and their clothes and little things like hairs on their legs—and the next day they're all burned up and dead. I'm left wondering how their burned up body must look, what burned up eyeballs look like. What about the hair on their legs? *And where are they now?*

It's all so peculiar and made worse by the fact that no one talks to me about it. Somehow I get a sense that my fiery death pain is linked to something much, much bigger, but I don't know how I know this or what bigger thing it could be. I'm confused about it all, especially how everything makes me feel.

The mother doesn't discuss it. She's in a hurry. When the neighbor, Mr. Owen, died, the mother came home early, then she drove to his house for the funeral. Before she left she told me they *cremated* his body.

"What does that mean?"

She's running late, of course. I stand at the door to her bedroom that I'm forbidden to enter. Her words come out muffled and waspish as she tries to hold her lips still so she won't smear lipstick in unwanted places.

"They burn the body and throw the ashes into the sea," she says with a final smack.

An aerosol application to a perfectly coiffed crown and a snap of the purse and the mother is out the door. I stand, dazed, staring at the wall. *What?*

In her wake, I walk over to the sliding glass door, open it, walk out onto the deck and look in the direction of Mr. Owen's homestead by the ocean. I imagine an old man's body, lying flat on a scaffold of sticks while people surround him and watch as the whole motif is consumed by raging flames.

Maybe this is how they do it in Hawaii. There is a lot of time to ponder such mysteries while we ride in the car to Hilo.

The mother drops us off at the new Hilo Mall and heads to work. She'll meet us for lunch at Kress or Penney's where waitresses kindly toast my hotdog bun, making it the most delicious thing I've ever tasted.

We've got a whole day and it's really much too long for children to be on their own without any place to rest or no parental supervision, but this is the way the mother does things.

I peruse the aisles of Kress, back and forth, bleary eyed with a burgeoning gluttony for *things*: lipstick, necklaces, lotions; aisle after aisle of alluring temptations all vying for my heart and my enormous sum of fifteen dollars. I spend every single cent because I find it imperative to pay homage to the source of my newfound joyfulness. It rides on the wings of new stuff.

At the end of the mother's day, she pilots the car up to the pre-appointed location and Sarah, Adam, and I penetrate the already thick cloud of blue. Sinking low in the backseat, we travel toward the duplicitous familiarity of her house in Hawaiian Paradise Park.

I'm nursing a terrible headache, the result of a day spent sniffing perfumes and eating too much candy. I'm trying to immobilize my skull to keep it from exploding.

The mother makes a brief stop at the Keaau post office. She leaves her burning cigarette in the ashtray. The blue ribbon snakes its way sideways and upward until it crashes against the car's inner shell and bounces back in little squiggles.

"Did I get anything?" Sarah hollers out the window to an emerging mother grasping a bundle of envelopes.

"Just a minute," the mother spits as she climbs back into the driver's seat. She grabs the idle cigarette and brings it to her hungry mouth and the blue ribbon follows obediently. She then hands Sarah two large manila envelopes.

"Oh, goodie!" Sarah about jumps up and down in her seat. This is unusual for her, because she's very even-keeled. She's been writing to the

TV stars and they're sending back autographed pictures. Sometimes they'll be small postcard-sized black and whites with pre-printed autographs, but more often they're full eight by ten glossy colored photos with "To Sarah, Best Wishes, Sandy Duncan" or some other TV notable. None of us thought Sarah would have this much success, but the pictures keep coming. When she gets home she'll mount each of her acquisitions in the pages of her photo album, which just fuels her desire for more so she'll send off a few more requests and keep track of everything. Sarah is very organized.

The mother takes a drag, replaces her cigarette, and tears open the side of an envelope.

I study her. Inquisitions about the adult world roll off my tongue in rapid succession. Everything is so nebulous and arcane, so close and yet so distant. The mother is careful, always, about what she says, revealing what seems to me to be as little as possible. I don't understand why she finds my curiosity so reprehensible, my presence so daunting.

Steady and adroit, manicured fingers perform her mysterious procedures, always predictable, always flawlessly executed.

I can't help but wonder if someday I'll be a mother driving my kids around, writing checks at the grocery store, stopping at the post office, cigarette in the ashtray. I doubt it. The idea is just too preposterous to contemplate.

She takes yet another drag and returns her cigarette to the ashtray. The blue line floats upward, interrupted occasionally by an invisible puff of air, undoubtedly coming from the car's open window. Bullied sideways for just a second like some kind of dance, it resumes its posture until my bored breath interrupts it again and then again.

The manipulation is entertaining and, by free association, my mind is instantly back on Hollis Street. The mother is seated in her chair, reading, her faithful blue companion ascending.

I ponder imponderables: Is the ribbon angry because my breath interrupts its upward travel? Will it come back to get me later, when I don't expect it, because I made it mad? Will it rage like the father or the Hawaiian kids or burn me up when the mother drives too fast?

I wish the mother would hurry up. Although it's only been a few minutes, it feels like hours as my head undulates in out of squeezing pain. It always does this. Intolerable torture followed by an easing up that I always mistake for a permanent waning. But a few seconds later, it's back with a vengeance and I'm cradling my head once more, trying to mentally distance myself from the excruciating ache.

She reads the folded envelope contents, twirls a clump of her hair through her fingers, grabs the cigarette again, breathes, puts it back, and twirls and reads. It's all very mysterious and predictable—her world, off limits to me.

Without a preamble, she tosses the papers aside, pulls the car out of the lot, and heads for Hawaiian Paradise Park.

So this wad of folded papers, of obvious importance to the mother, sits mysteriously by the mother's bulging purse. When the migraine monster pulls back yet again, up pops the familiar compulsion to rummage through it, to see what the mother deems important enough to tote around everywhere. Five minutes is all I need. I want to see all the cool stuff the mother doesn't want me to see stuffed inside her purse. Wrigley's spearmint gum, undoubtedly. Lipstick, checkbook ….

***

With TV as my teacher, I'm gaining a burgeoning knowledge of adult activities. I like to mentally chronicle the mother's evening exploits. She meets suitors at the "nightclubs" on Banyan Drive. She's dolled up and beautiful, her scarlet lips perfectly matching her painted fingernails. Her coiffed hair, her white teeth and her Windsong perfume—perfection.

She's seated at the dimly lit bar having drinks and smiling, dignified, somewhat guarded but friendly, cigarette cradled between her long fingers. She's flirting with a Michael Douglas-looking man and maybe they'll end up in bed together like the ladies do on TV and maybe that is why she doesn't come home sometimes.

There are probably a lot of dates that don't pass muster and don't graduate to visiting rights at the mother's home in Hawaiian Paradise Park. Plus, because she's ashamed of Sarah, Adam, and me and our messy surroundings, she's careful about who she brings here. It's going to take a special guy to win her over after being jilted so many times, especially by the father who not only jilted her but saddled her with three unruly kids.

Her night life is a place she can forget about it all, drink and be merry and meet a nice man.

Enter Boyd, the mother's bewildering choice for a husband. He's Hawaiian with a bald head and macro-girth. He's twenty years her senior and a harbinger of bad things to come.

CHAPTER SEVEN

As my callused bare feet stride painlessly over gravel, I quell an impulse to show off. It's pretty cool being this impervious to sharp things. If only the rest of me were as tough as my feet.

"Look at that line," I comment to Willa as we begin to make our way past a longer-than-usual backup of cars waiting to buy gas.

"Yeah, it's the energy crisis," Willa says with confidence.

Although I don't voice it, I can't help but wonder how people waiting for gas is linked to a *crisis*. Sarah might be able to explain it if I think to ask her. She probably won't, though. I annoy her.

As we pass the fish market I'm assaulted by a familiar stench that reminds me to hold my breath and walk quickly. The mystery behind the energy crisis pales in comparison to the thought of people eating stuff that smells this bad, but Hawaiians eat some pretty unappetizing foods.

Stepping onto the dusty boardwalk, Willa and I turn the corner and we're immediately under the surveillance of a mute, ancient Japanese man, keeping vigil at his post. Maybe he doesn't speak English.

Eyeing me suspiciously, he takes my coins and turns to open his cash register. Like most adults, he doesn't like me but he likes Willa because she's Hawaiian. Small-town Hawaii is clannish. Everyone knows everyone else's children and they call the ladies "Auntie" even when they're not related.

Snippets of various conversations are going in and out of my consciousness as a group of us waits for our afternoon bus ride.

"School's *pau*. You no can do it already."

Now that I've been in Hawaii for three years, I've become accustomed to the blending of English and Hawaiian and even learned several Hawaiian words. Sarah and I toss insults back and forth because we each sound ridiculous to the other when we talk in pidgin like the locals.

Many of the kids, including Willa, head across the street to one of the impoverished, rusticated houses where some "Auntie" teaches *catechism*. That's got something to do with the Bible. At first I felt a little bit left out but now I don't care. I just want to get on the bus and go home.

"Spock ya lata, man," yells a high school boy out his car's window. His words, somewhat overshadowed by his radio blaring, "Lou-ee, Lou-ee, Lou-ee, Lou-ee-ee …" are intended for a group of younger boys gathered in a dusty clearing on the side of the road. They stop their "rock, paper, scissors" and wave back. I can see marbles in their cupped hands as the high school boy's car takes off with an earsplitting rumble and reignites my smoldering anxiety. Instinctively, I look up and glare at the clouds, willing away any inkling of a thunderstorm.

Waiting for the bus allows me a little more time to examine my next set of perplexities: my growing attraction to the bus driver. There is something about him that makes me *want* him. I fantasize about him being interested in me and touching me. He consumes me. It's like a separate me that I have no control over, a movie playing in my mind that doesn't have an off switch.

Sometimes I look at him while he drives the bus and I swear he's looking right at me in his up-above mirror. But he's got sunglasses on so I can't really tell. And then I remember that I'm nobody, just an ugly *haole*, the scum on the bottom of the gene pool. Why would anyone be interested in me?

Boarding the bus, I labor to divert my gawking, hungry eyes from the driver. I find my seat and sit silently while the din swirls around me. I'm unable to relate to so much of it—the desires and goals and antics of my classmates. They probably wouldn't understand me, either, like why I would have unrelenting amorous fantasies about a man who is probably old enough to be my father.

As the bus starts to move, I make what I think is eye contact with the driver and it's an electric, magnetic connection I've formed with him. Out of the blue, a thought occurs: Maybe *he* formed it with me. Maybe this is all the bus driver's doing and I'm just following his lead and maybe it will actually lead somewhere. On one level this seems enticing and exciting and illicit. Like maybe we could make out in the bushes somewhere. On another level, it scares me to death because he's so much older than me and I don't know if I want him touching me. Yet I want him to notice me and rescue me. Maybe he could be my *Too Sir, With Love,* I muse, replaying the song's gentle melody in my mind. Maybe he'll rescue me and love me. I can't keep thinking about that song, though, because it touches something deep inside me and I get teary-eyed.

Seated here on the bus with a boisterous cargo, I'm in my own world, lost in the crowd as I feel the electricity, the magnetic pull to the man up front. He *will* rescue me. He's a man. Maybe he can see the welts on my legs and arms and knows that the stepfather is a *bastard*, a term I quickly adopted after Sarah's initial use of it. Maybe he will finally declare that enough is enough and will rescue me. I don't want him to see the welts. I just want him to rescue me.

Without thinking, I break one of my cardinal rules, drawing attention to myself as I rise off my seat and quickly scan the heads in front of me. Adam is not hard to spot since he's one of the few boys with blonde hair. Yes, he's here, sitting with Jeremy.

Sarah? She's sitting with Lynette, which I find odd because it wasn't that long ago that Lynette and Sarah were arch enemies.

"I'm going to kick your fucking ass as soon as the bus gets to school, you fat ass haole bitch," Lynette screeched in non-negotiable decibels one morning a few months ago.

I kept thinking that Sarah could probably easily kick Lynette's ass since Sarah is much bigger and rage runs in our family.

When we got to school that day, the bus driver stopped the bus, got up, and stood outside. He didn't really say a whole lot—but he didn't need to. He just stood there like a guardsman protector. I bet he understood that his presence alone was enough to curtail any violence. Maybe this is why I fantasize about him rescuing me. He's strong and in control and must like kids since he drives this bus all over the place.

He systematically closes the door, checks his mirrors, and, as the bus sneezes and coughs, he moves it forward. I'm *finally* on my way home, away from this godforsaken school and all its assorted entrapments.

As I glance outside, someone plops down beside me. It's Lance, a thin, wiry, darker than dark-skinned Hawaiian boy in my class. He always smells slightly of poop and makes no apology for being quick with the hands. I push him away as often as he tries but he just giggles and tries again and my boobs hurt because sometimes he pinches them too hard before I can slap his hand.

Lance's home is a squalid compound situated just off the main highway right outside of town: a rusty tin roof; peeling paint; muddy yard; free ranging chickens; barking, scabby dogs; leaning fences; clothes hanging from the rickety porch railing; and at least a dozen brothers and sisters.

Despite his myriad annoying ways, I sort of like Lance. He used to have a rabid temper that frightened me and sometimes I would explode and try to kill him. But he's mellowed now and he seems to like me. And when people are nice to me, I'm nice back. I'm bred for this.

The bus driver taxis us north along the highway. He looks up in his mirror now and then and I glance toward him, making eye contact which fuels another surge of electricity.

Where the highway intersects with Makuu Drive, the bus driver pulls over and opens the door. A lot of kids get off at our stop now. I remember when it was just Sarah, Adam, and me.

***

As my bike's tires glide through one of the bare ruts along 31st Avenue, I see the mother's house coming into view. Adam is in the driveway, fussing with his bike, while Precious, our dog, looks up at me and starts wagging her tail.

"Are they in a good mood?" I ask Adam giving Precious the love she craves.

"No. You didn't clean the kitchen."

I shoo a persistent fly trying to land on one of the many sores sprinkled like paint on Adam's ankles. My own ankles look about the same. I don't know how they get there, these round, puss-filled wounds. Maybe they're bug bites that get inadvertently scratched while we're asleep. I'll just wake up in the morning and have a bunch of new round sores on my ankles. They look ugly and it seems to take forever for them to heal.

"I thought it was Sarah's day. Crap," I reply to a disinterested Adam.

The stepfather sits on the sofa, eyes glued to the TV. I can tell he's wearing his golfing clothes. When he sits in those shorts, they get tight around his lap and reveal a mass of scrotum off to one side. It's the kind of thing I want to look at because it's so bizarre and I don't want to look at because it's so bizarre. Boyd's presence makes me bristle and wish I could just escape somehow.

The mother is making dinner. She doesn't speak to me, which is typical. I look at the table and see that it's empty. From the looks of things, dinner is almost ready so I walk to the sink, wash my hands, and then open the silverware drawer. Usually the mother has to bark at me but tonight I just do it, and instead of infusing this task with ample bickering, I'm mute, just like the mother.

Behind the plates, a dead cockroach lays belly-up with its legs frozen in their last movements. I ignore it. There are so many cockroaches that I've grown used to them. At night when I turn on the light, they'll scatter under whatever they can find, and it doesn't even bother me anymore. Once I saw a large one in my closet, nestled in my bathrobe. That was going too far. I shivered and screamed and now I shake all of my clothes before I put them on.

Dinner is cooked and served to please Boyd's discriminating palate. Hawaiian cuisine looks to me like regurgitated barf. I have no stomach for it. But it's probably just the negative associations. The food likely wouldn't taste all that bad if I was a happy person.

There is no pleasant dinner conversation, just people sitting around the table, angry at each other for a variety of reasons. The only one who isn't mad is Adam and that's because he's too young to understand. I know he feels caught between loyalty to his life-giving mother and alliance with his battle-scarred sisters.

After dinner, it's up to Sarah or me to do the dishes while the mother sits on the sofa with the stepfather, smokes a cigarette, nurses an after-dinner drink and reads the paper. She tells us in her pithy tone that she's entitled to a little relaxation after a long day and that it wouldn't kill Sarah and me to help out around here.

I see her sitting there and I resent that I'm working while she's relaxing. I slam things around and I leave little bits of food on the dishes, not on purpose but because I don't care. I'm not paying attention and I'm pissed off that she sits there while I slave away. It's not fair that she makes me do all this.

I just want this kitchen clean-up servitude to be over with and, when it is, I stomp off to the bedroom. I start to close the door, but Boyd pipes up.

"Leave it open," he thunders in his pidgin parlance.

I seethe, and slam the door back against the wall, likely causing a dent. Slightly rueful, I retreat to the one spot in the room where he can't see me from his vantage point on the sofa.

Sarah is sitting on her bed, engaged in homework. The radio is turned down but I can still hear snippets of "The Lion Sleeps Tonight" and the ridiculous song just adds to my already pissed off state.

"This is so wrong," I whisper loudly. "We can't even have privacy in our own bedroom. God, I wish he would *die*." I sit on my bed and kick my legs a few times to vent. The mother and Boyd can probably hear me, but I don't care.

Sarah, always the wiser, ignores me. I stand, walk to the window. Outside in the waning daylight, the knee-high grass is jostled by a slight wind. It's probably infested with a gazillion praying mantises, I think, trying to distract myself from my misery. They *fly* and sometimes land on my head. Not to be outdone, the fist-sized spiders seem to relish their prominence by appearing high on the wall, at bedtime. Bugs are *big* in Hawaii — and I hate them.

I don't get very far into my entomological reflection before Boyd barges into the room wielding his signature weapon, a section of Adam's Hot Wheels track. Immediately a blur of orange is slamming into my bare legs and arms, across my face.

"I told you to leave the door open, goddamn it! Why don't you do as I say, you filthy little goddamned brat?"

I'm on the floor, legs flailing mostly at nothing but occasionally serving a wallop on my archest of enemies.

"I hate your guts, you bastard," I scream, refusing the role of powerless victim. In the beginning I wouldn't have dared such brazenness but it didn't take long to learn that his venom would be just as potent regardless. And somehow my refusal to cower allows me to hang on to a nebulous tuft of dignity.

Between blows he retorts, "I hate you, too, you selfish little pig. You brat, you bitchy goddamned brat!"

I'm crying but it's not a mournful, repentant cry. It's a hysterical, frenzied, furious cry. I've lost control and tears stream down my face and mix with my hair and snot and temporarily blind me.

I scream, "I hate you" again.

He's bigger. He drops the Hot Wheels track and grabs my hair and slaps my skin with a stinging crack and gathers his hand into a fist and lets loose. I'm gone until I detect his winded fatigue.

"Leave … the goddamned … door open … or I'll be back… to finish you off. You hear me?" he bellows between breaths, pointing his fat Hawaiian finger at me, then heaving my body back against the wall to force eye contact.

Prohibited from private crying and recuperation, Boyd's humiliating open-door mandate is strictly enforced, shoving any vestiges of dignity over the cliff into oblivion. From somewhere inside my vast cache of resentment, I sense that Boyd feels justified with his violence. It's his duty. The only way I'll become a good person—a compliant, cheerful, grateful, nebbish robot—is if he beats the *bad* out of me. If he doesn't, I'm destined for delinquency. I'll grow up and be a murderer or rob banks.

But that would imply that he actually cared about my future. I'm positive he doesn't. His violence is about his freedom to wield power, an opportunity to ignite his short fuse on a defenseless target.

Perhaps the mother needs a rescuer, too. Or maybe Boyd's violence is a huge turn-on and the two of them make great love later on. Who knows?

My tears coalesce with two steady streams of snot and my face is beyond saturated. I grab the hem of my shirt and wipe my nose and push back the wet hair plastered against my face. Involuntary gasps of air somehow make it to my lungs and help me to calm down. They serve to release the deeper tears, the tears of entrapment, the deep, visceral agony. Years later I'll discover the exact definition: *Despair*. But as a thirteen-year-old, I can't figure out what's going on, can't identify and understand this gargantuan gloom. My ignorance makes the whole thing all that much worse.

And my self-hatred is at an all time high. I wish I could die. That might be my only escape.

Sitting on my bed, I struggle to regain some sense of humanity. A brief flash of the bus driver shimmies through my brain. He's far away, probably with his own family. I'm sure now that he'll never really know the hellhole I live in. Truthfully, I don't want him to know because it's so awful and if he knew he'd never rescue me.

He never will rescue me. The whole thing is just a stupid lie I tell myself to keep from going insane.

Sarah and Adam have endured the same beatings, verbatim. I hate hearing their screams and his yelling and hearing the slapping and the thumping as their bodies are thrown around. It incites this odd combination of rage and helplessness.

I can hear the TV from the ear that isn't pressed into my pillow. It's hard to miss when the door is wide open in such a small house. Eventually I drift off to sleep and wake to the familiar rhythmic moaning. Usually I ignore it, roll over and go back to sleep. But tonight I have the wherewithal to investigate.

The door to the mother's room is also wide open. I glance around the corner and see the mother's bare upraised knees and Boyd's large body between them moving and moaning.

I've seen enough.

Silently crawling back into bed, I hold onto an infinitesimal ray of hope for the bus driver and how badly I need him. I wonder if I'll ever get the nerve to actually *talk* to him. I want to but I'm too scared.

"Children of the Night" on Sarah's Stylistics album churns in my head and I want to cry because of all the sadness but I have no tears left.

Nighttime is ominous. I always hear footsteps and sometimes I'll see a dull illumination on the wall. And there is no one to talk to about how scared I am.

Sometimes at night the whole house will shake violently. It's an earthquake brought on by the constant activity of the volcano about thirty miles away. Even the most benign recollection of such traumas has the power to pull me back into a state of raw, inconsolable fear.

The worst event occurred at school. In seconds, ordinary gave way to the jerking and surging of a rollercoaster and the thunderous cacophony of a freight train. It rumbled under my body for what seemed like an eternity. Mr. Woodward must have noticed other students outside and maybe he was worried that the building was going to crumble because he yelled, "Get outside!"

By the time we stumbled onto the grass the rumbling stopped.

We went back to our desks and Mr. Woodward continued his math lesson like nothing had happened. Rob and I looked at each other with equal bewilderment, like Mr. Woodward was a complete moron.

The wall of bricks that closes out the world had imploded upon me that day and a helpless infant had emerged. I couldn't really comprehend what I was seeing. My surroundings seemed miles away rather than a few inches and everything felt like it was in slow motion *and* fast forward. I laid my head on my desk. I could feel my moist breath. Until I heard "earthquake" I wasn't sure what had happened. It made me sleepy.

And I'm sleepy now. There is no more rumbling. There is no more moaning and I'm not listening to the footsteps. They're still there but I'm not listening.

CHAPTER EIGHT

"Do this block and the next and I'll pick you up at the end of the street in one hour," the mother commands Sarah and me through the car window. Then she drives off with Adam. I assume they'll be passing out the stepfather's flyers on some other block. Sarah and I are stuck here going from house to house, walking up to the front door and dropping these stupid printed papers off, telling people to vote for Boyd.

The neighborhood is quiet and peaceful. The yards are well-groomed and the houses are painted tidy colors like white and light brown. This whole block reminds me a little bit of Oregon except that I can see Hilo Bay in the distance and there are palm trees and tikis in front of many of the houses.

Boyd has been dabbling in politics and the mother thinks that Sarah, Adam, and I should jump on the bandwagon and cheer him on and rah rah rah. But passing out these flyers—resentfully, at that—is the best Sarah and I can do. It's really hard to do nice things for someone who habitually beats me. I remind myself that Boyd is just trying to get me to "straighten up" and has to take drastic measures because I'm so bad.

I suppose the safest way to be fatherly is to offer gifts. One day Boyd brought home a whole box of Scholastic paperback books. I remember how shocked I was. I thought maybe they were for someone else, or some project or something, certainly not for Adam and Sarah and me. The mother wanted me to be sure and thank Boyd. *Wow, books!*

Sorting through the colored covers, I didn't see anything that interested me. I told myself that I wasn't a book person anyway.

"Read this one, you'll like it," Sarah said, handing me *Ghost Town Treasure.*

I thumbed through the pictures several times and it looked interesting so I finally conceded. The protagonists, a group of young explorers, found a message that said "gold in the cave" so they went searching for it. But eventually they found out the message really said, "*cold* in the cave."

Sarah was right, it was a good story and I liked it. But it didn't get me interested in the other books. Maybe because I'd already learned the lesson that getting excited about something good, and then going in search of it usually led me to the realization that the "good" maybe wasn't what I'd thought—and maybe not good at all

I was more interested in the mother's cedar chest and one day while the mother and Boyd were gone I rummaged through it and found the mother's wedding album. I took a pen and scribbled mustaches on the black and white pictures of her and the father and the extended family.

They aren't married anymore, I reasoned. And besides, the mother doesn't even like the father, so what's the difference?

Then, after more digging, I discovered the mother's Eastern Star Bible. I wrote all over it, too.

When the mother discovered that I had ruined her stuff, she and Boyd got a padlock and one of those hinged metal things that has a narrow hole in it so the loop, mounted to the door, can go through it. The padlock secures it all and, voila, a locked door. Now every time they leave, they lock the door. It looks kind of stupid there, that lock on the door that hides all the mother's secret stuff that she doesn't want her bratty kid to desecrate.

The mother has all kinds of cool things locked behind that door. She's an attractive woman and likes to primp herself. Her mirrored vanity holds a bunch of trinkets and toiletries like Windsong perfume and lots of nail polishes and lotions and lipsticks and stuff young girls like to look at and try out. The mother doesn't want her kids touching her stuff so she locks the door when she leaves. And she's oblivious to the message she's sending.

Sarah and I wait at the corner for the mother, having canvassed all of the houses on this block and the one before that, except for a house with a mean-looking dog.

"I'm so tired and thirsty. Where are we going now?" I say to the mother.

"We'll get groceries and then head for home," the mother says as restorative air rushes across my face through the open window.

Grocery shopping? This surprises me because the mother hates to take Adam, Sarah, and me shopping. We constantly bug her about buying this and buying that. Maybe today she figures we'll be too tired to bother with the begging.

When we get to the frozen food aisle the mother says, "Okay, pick out some TV dinners."

I go for the Mexican style because they remind me of the grandma thousands of miles away. Her enchiladas were so delicious, I remember, as I stand and stare at the boxes behind the glass. Banquet or Swanson?

Does this mean you're leaving?" Sarah asks. I wonder if she's aware that she sounds rude.

"Yes, Boyd and I will be gone for three days."

"Where are you going?" Adam asks. I think I detect just a tiny bit of sadness in his voice.

"Honolulu," she says without elaborating.

She apparently didn't detect any sadness in Adam. I'm sure she didn't detect any sadness in Sarah or me, either, because our sadness is buried under a pile of rubble. Neither of us lets on how glad we are about our impending freedom.

"What are you going to do there?" Adam wants to know. I can detect anxiety in his voice and I bet he's hoping for some kind of relief.

The mother pushes the cart along and doesn't answer. It's her world and the kids aren't allowed into it. That's one of her signatures. Like the lock on her door that keeps us out of her bedroom, we're kept out of the things she does and the people she sees. It's all very cryptic and mysterious and not meant for children to know about

As the mother turns onto another aisle, Sarah holds back, grabs my arm and whispers, "yippee."

I let out a giggle more for Sarah's benefit than mine. Then I whisper the thought that just raced into my head. "What if she makes us stay at Grandma's?"

"If she was going to make us stay with Grandma, do you think she'd be buying us TV dinners, stupid?"

I don't have to answer the obvious so I just reply with a sheepish, "Oh, yeah."

Sarah's right, as usual. Her being better than me all the time really pisses me off and normally I would hit or kick her for putting me down, but I'm too tired and now I have something to look forward to. So I just move on.

"Can we get cereal, too?" I ask, hoping the mother's generosity—or guilt—will be her guide.

"Okay."

I grab a box of "Buckwheats" and toss it into the cart.

The mother and stepfather take a lot of trips now. The mother used to make us stay with the mean grandma and mean grandpa. But not long after the mean grandpa died, she started letting us stay alone. Each time it's basically the same procedure. She stocks up on plenty of pre-packaged food items. She and Boyd leave in the morning and, a few hours before they're due back, we run around and clean up all the messes we made while they were gone.

***

The mother drives up 31st Avenue then turns onto the driveway of her house in Hawaiian Paradise Park. And there it is, the white freezer front, exposed.

"Dang. We left the freezer closet open again," I mutter under my breath.

Closing the car door, I trot over and pull the sliding brown door to conceal the freezer but Sarah pipes up, "Why are you closing that? We've got a bunch of stuff to put in there, dummy."

I push the door back open. "We're supposed to close this when we leave," I vent to no one since they're all carrying groceries up the steps and into the house.

"Get Precious' dog food out of the back," the mother yells.

Precious has a sense about these things. She's wagging her tail, happy to have us home, and I've ignored her as usual. I grab the bag and she's right there, tender eyes looking up at me, hoping I'll fill her bowl. Prissy comes running, too, so I find her food and fill the water. This is Adam's job and right then he walks out.

"You didn't leave out any water for Precious or Prissy," I say, assaulting him with verbal bullets that are indicative of my emotional turmoil and unhappiness. Adam doesn't need or deserve my bullshit but he's young and he's an easy target and I'm an idiot.

***

It's a school day, but Sarah and I have already decided we're skipping. We whispered it over last night while listening to the radio. Bill Withers was singing, "Ain't no sunshine when she's gone ..." and I was thinking, you got that right, buddy. I live in Hawaii—paradise—but there ain't no sunshine around here. Only darkness every day.

Of course, the radio was too loud. "Turn that down," the mother and Boyd bellowed alternately in response to Sarah and me alternately inching it back up. We were hoping they'd tire of the stupid open-door mandate and allow us some privacy. No such luck. Eventually it escalated to, "Turn that *damn* thing down, goddamn it!"

Sarah and I are getting ready for school, going through the motions to ensure there is nothing out of the ordinary. I can hear the coffee pot burping in the kitchen. The mother and Boyd are in their bedroom, packing their stuff. I can hear Boyd's deep voice mumbling something and the mother's clear lady voice answering back. They're getting ready to leave.

At the appointed time, we say goodbye with no fanfare, and no hugs or kisses but I don't think twice about this, since it never happens anyway. We make our way down 31st Avenue to Makuu Drive. Usually we walk all the way to the highway where the bus pulls over so we can get on. But today we make Adam go on while Sarah and I duck into the bushes where we'll be able to see the mother's car when she and Boyd drive by.

I quell the rising anxiety for the sake of our plan.

"Will we get caught?" The baby me wants to know.

"Who is going to find us?" The older me retorts. This older me, of course, is the voice of Sarah in me—wiser, stronger, more confident, more rebellious, fearless. I want Sarah-me to dominate but she's always overpowered by Baby-me—the scared, anxiety ridden little girl who needs somebody to rescue her.

I wonder if the bus driver will miss me, if I even matter at all to him, and, if I do, will he ever rescue me? Sarah-me chides Baby-me for being so silly and childish but I can't stop the thoughts and the hope.

Crouching down, Sarah and I hide like criminals eluding police, listening for the mother's Mazda to drive by so we can walk home.

With a cramp forming in my ankle, I surrender my tentative squatting to a full-fledged repose. Much better.

The grass is taller than I am and it looks strange from this vantage point, tall and pointy and moving ever so slightly in the morning breeze.

A few feet away is a small clump of orchid foliage. I scan it, checking for flowers, then instinctively reach down to a small clump of leaves, the ones that magically close up when I run my finger along them. They're hiding, too, shy little things. It amazes me that they can survive here along this arid roadside. I should be more like this silly little plant that grows in this inhospitable place. Why am I so ungrateful and unwilling to thrive?

I'm having doubts about everything right now.

Sarah's voice breaks my melancholy and replaces it with full-on fear. It's too late now. I'm sure the bus has already come. I'm committed to my delinquency.

"Listen, I think I hear it," she says.

Yes, there is definitely the sound of tires rolling over gravel and it's getting closer. But there are lots of cars that travel along this road so I'd better not get too excited and jump out and reveal myself and have hell to pay. Wait and watch.

"Yep. There they go," I say, trying to mimic Sarah.

"It's about damn time," Sarah's words are a mixture of bliss and bitterness. She's already back on the road before I'm standing. My "wait for me" falls on deaf ears. I've forgotten about checking for orchids.

***

Skipping school is remarkably simple and the process gets easier with every undertaking. The mother doesn't even look at the "Days Absent" on the report card, or, if she does, she ignores it. Being home, away from mean school kids, has its allure. I don't have to worry all the time about getting called names and getting pinched or hit. In fact, skipping school is more than just alluring, it's vital.

Sometimes after school while I'm waiting for the bus, I won't see Adam. I start to panic before realizing that he's skipped school all by himself. This worries me but when I think about it, how can I blame Adam for not wanting to go to school where he'll just get into a fight with some Hawaiian kid? Or maybe he's figured out how to torment back and hates himself for it like I hate myself for tormenting him.

I like being here alone where I can eat, watch TV, daydream, do whatever I want.

Right next to my opened—always—bedroom door is the mother's locked door and I'm thinking I'd like to break in. I can't pick this lock, but I bet I could go outside and crawl in through the window. Then I could see what she's got in there that she's so worried about me destroying.

I touch the lock, swing and twirl it around with my finger. It makes a hollow thud when I accidentally let it hit the door. I wonder why … why everything. Lots of questions, no answers, just boredom. But at least when I skip school, I don't have to listen to everyone else's questions.

Seated by the window in the bedroom Sarah and I share, I'm picturing a sliding glass door and a deck instead of a confining window. The mean grandma has one in her condo in Hilo. It looks out over Hilo Bay. It's very pretty.

There's no way I would tell the mother about my vision because she'd either ignore me or offer a dismissive "We can't afford it" if perchance she was in a good enough mood to even answer. I ought to give up the notion of trying to better my world but from some intangible place inside my being, there is a tiny seed of optimism and creativity and a need to make things beautiful and pleasant and peaceful. Like things are in Hilo and in Kailua at the Kona Hilton.

The Kona side of the island is where the tourists go and everything is lovely for them. Even the Pacific Ocean is calm and warm and inviting, not nearly as scary as it is on Hilo's windward side where we live and where the volcano keeps things interesting.

The Kona Hilton is a curved cement high-rise painted white and surrounded by a jungle of tropical greenery and cascading waterfalls. The mother and Boyd took us to see it.

Our hotel room had a sliding glass door and a deck—okay, *lanai*— that looked out upon the waters of Kailua Bay and this is what I want for my bedroom. My lanai doesn't have to look out upon beautiful waters or anything. It can just look out on the backyard with its weeds and grass and Ohia and that would be okay because it would be *my* place. I'd have a pot with pretty flowers or something, maybe a plumeria plant that would grow big enough to offer some shade. I could pick the fragrant flowers and string them into a lei like Sarah and Adam and I used to do when we first came to Hawaii. When things look pretty it makes it easier to put up with all the unpleasant things.

The early afternoon sun warms my face as I look out the window and think about Kailua and swimming in the hotel's pool. Adam was in the shallow end all by himself with a little toy floater and I thought I could hear him talking quietly to himself, which made me realize that he's alone almost all the time when he's not playing with Jeremy. I feel a mixture of incomprehensible emotions for Adam. I want to protect him but I'm powerless. I want to embrace him and climb into his world and guide him somehow, but I don't know where to take him or how to get there. I guess this is love but I'm not really sure.

Adam used to like to play with the cousins from the mainland. When the scary aunt and the scary uncle came to Hawaii it was weird to see them but Adam probably liked having someone to do things with.

I didn't know how to deal with Norbert so I overcompensated by becoming a complete know-it-all. My general attitude was "I know all about Hawaii and you don't, so there." Norbert was my nemesis while I was in his world. Now that he was in mine, it was payback time.

But I was still oblivious to the true impetus for my anger and because payback wasn't really a reality, I retreated to my room and locked the door.

The mother and the mean grandma drove the scary aunt and the scary uncle and all of us kids up to the volcano. We walked Chain of Craters Road to see how the lava flowed right over it, making it impossible to drive.

"You're not supposed to take any of the lava because it pisses off Madame Pele," I announced to Norbert. "And if you piss her off, bad things will happen to you."

I wasn't sure if he was listening but *I* was and my words made me wonder if I'd taken some lava and just didn't remember it. That could explain why bad things seem to happen to me so much.

So for the duration of the hike down Chain of Craters Road with a vast wasteland of lava in the distance and the familiar band of blue ocean beyond that, I tried to think back to a time when I might have confiscated Pele's precious lava. Maybe if I could put the lava back, my life would make a turn for the better.

***

Sarah and I—and probably Adam, too—really enjoy it when the mother and Boyd go away for a few days. I suppose it should matter that I don't have a Brady Bunch mother but the wound is dark and lonesome and courses its venom through my veins. It's a familiar fact of my life. And making herself so elusive is actually my saving grace. It gives me the freedom I need to survive.

But when the mother and Boyd are home, it's hell. The beatings continue right up until the end.

"I hate you, you bastard," I scream to preserve myself. "I can't wait to go back to the mainland."

"I can't wait, either. I can't wait … for you … to be out of here … you goddamned filthy brat … so I can live … in peace and quiet!"

I let the scalding shower water pour over my bruises and welts to reinforce and magnify the sting—to punish myself. Despite my seething rage, I know I deserve all of this because I refuse to entertain the mother's "straighten up" mandate. I'm too angry. Despite the stepfather's corporal attempts, I disdain the mere notion of compliance so I'm getting exactly what I deserve. Every welt and bruise is a direct result of my willful defiance.

***

The mother wrote to the father explaining that on June 16th, after school lets out, she'll be sending Sarah and me back to the mainland to live with him.

The mother purchases "standby" airline tickets. I don't get what this means so Sarah explains. "It means that if the plane is too full, we'll have to sit and wait for another flight. It won't be a problem in Hilo, but it might be in Honolulu." Then, out of earshot, "She's cheap and doesn't want to spend her money on the full fare."

Adam isn't going with us. I can't let myself think about how awful it will be for him when Boyd's rage is exclusively unleashed on him. It hurts too much. Poor Adam. I want to love him but I don't know how.

Maybe the mother and Boyd feel that once Sarah and I are gone, Adam will "straighten up," or maybe they're worried that my rage will escalate to the point where I kill him.

Whatever the reasons, my separation from Adam will be permanent, and so will the pain.

***

Shockingly out of character, the mother drives Sarah and me to Hilo. At Penney's, she lets us each pick out a new outfit to wear on the plane. Unable to grasp the mother's present inconsistencies, I go along. I choose a halter sundress with a white collar because this is what's in style right now.

Packing the suitcase doesn't take Sarah and me very long. I'm admittedly a bit saddened by having to leave all of my Barbie things, but I find my mood ring and my *puka* shells and record albums and 45s, and, of course, my diary. These items are small enough to fit in the suitcase.

On the ride to Hilo, we pass the curve where the car crash killed our friends. The grass that was black and burned for so long has grown back thick and green, completely disguising the reality of that horrendous night three years ago. Maybe this is what it will be like after I leave Hawaii. The grass will grow high and disguise this sick nightmare and it will be like it never happened.

The echo of voices swarming and bouncing off the walls fills up the airport's placid air. As I watch people canter back and forth, I contemplate the monumental change in front of me. Elated yet apprehensive, I've got to believe that, as I close off the worst part of my life, I'm opening the door to the best. Improvements, albeit invisible at this point, await. For one thing, I won't feel so trapped

While we wait to board the plane, I employ my amicability to ease the undeniable tension. Yet there's only so much that I can do and there are still too many silences. I suppose it's all been said but, tragically, *nothing* has been said. It's the end of an era, The Hawaii Era.

The mother sits, silent, smoking a cigarette. I want to take Adam in my arms and hold him but I'm paralyzed at the thought. I'm abandoning him. The horrendous guilt paints an excruciating black cloud over my excitement to be free.

As I feel the energy of the airplane's propulsion, I see the mother and Adam. They're turning to leave and now they're out of sight and I can't think about them anymore.

CHAPTER NINE

A sharp white line curves and bends to separate the island from the ocean. I can see it all far below as the airplane makes a gentle turn toward Oahu. This view is my final image of the Big Island.

I can feel the airplane's gentle forward motion as it journeys toward its destination. I'm not nervous yet. It's not until we reach cruising altitude and it feels like the plane is coasting that panic sets in. Then any sudden movement or sound gets me white-knuckled.

Snippets of quiet conversation mingle with the engine's drone. There are a lot of empty seats. Sarah, next to me, is leaning into the aisle and scanning both directions. Maybe there won't be that many people getting on in Honolulu so we can still have these seats.

Of course. we won't know until we get there, but so far, so good. It would have been nicer if we didn't have this "standby" uncertainty, but things are what they are and we're finally away from the Hawaii hell. It can only improve from now on.

A stewardess walks by and then turns back and asks if we need anything. I look at Sarah since she's older and she looks at me and then back at the lady and says, "No, we're fine, thank you," which is very polite.

Honolulu isn't very far away and the little bell already rang, but I didn't even take off my seat belt.

Sarah and I occupy two of the thousands of chairs in the Honolulu airport. I keep thinking there can't be any more people coming and then, as if on cue, another whole group will show up. I'm starting to get a little nervous. It's evening and we may need to sleep here overnight. I look for beds but all I see are people and these uncomfortable chairs.

We were assuming that since this is a red-eye there might not be very many passengers, but it looks like everyone in Honolulu is interested in going to Portland tonight. People continue to file in. Doing what we can to keep our spirits up, we console ourselves with the fact that the plane is a DC-10, which is pretty big, so it can fit a lot of people.

I see a man with a ukulele and this reminds me of the ukuleles Sarah, Adam and I had. I could only play C, F, and G but that was enough to fake it through parts of "Tiny Bubbles" or "Lahaina Luna."

Soon enough, Sarah and I are sitting in the same seats because the airport people took pity on us and saved them.

Directly in front of us, a man keeps trying to get the attention of the stewardess. He orders more drinks, laughing and calling her darling and sweetie. Lots of the other passengers are whooping it up, too—tourists going home, Sarah and I conclude. They're keeping a tight grip on their final vacation hours, until the soporific alcohol loosens it. Slowly the voices go mute as they drift off to sleep. Then it's quiet.

Sarah is asleep. She can relax and sleep on an airplane but I can't. I'm fidgety and restless. I can feel my heart beating and my hands are like ice. I don't really like floating through the air so high up and not knowing whether we might come down and drown in the Pacific Ocean because of a faulty engine. If we did, there would be no one to help us. All of these worst case scenarios seem to evade the thoughts of the sleeping passengers, while they haunt me. I keep listening for any little bump or sound, and doing so is keeping me from going to sleep. I'm sure this means something is wrong with me.

I wish I could go up there and talk to the pilots. Maybe they'd tell me I have nothing to worry about, that they've done this a thousand times, that the engines are not going to fail, that, statistically, flying is safer than driving. I'd love to have them comfort me but they're in their world and I'm in mine and I'm just riding along at their mercy and that of those engines. If I could, I'd sit on the floor right there by the door. Quietly I'd watch them and listen to them, absorb their confidence and fearlessness. Then I'd know I was okay. That's all I really want in life, to know I'm okay, but it's such an elusive thing.

I attempt to distract myself with pondering what lies ahead. Will Portland have any good radio stations and, if so, will they play the same songs I heard in Hawaii?

Back in April, when we were in Hilo shopping for Sarah's birthday, I saw the *Band on the Run* album. I wanted it but I didn't have enough money. The next day the mother brought it home for me. For the life of me I couldn't understand why she bought an album for *me* on Sarah's birthday. The whole thing was very peculiar but I didn't look a gift horse in the mouth and I didn't let myself think about how confusing it must have been for Sarah. I just played the album over and over and kind of fell in love with Paul McCartney.

I can see just a scintilla of red sky out my window: morning. It's June so the sun rises early. Pretty soon the sunshine is waking up the sleeping passengers as it streams in through the windows. Looking down, I see thick clouds and before long we're riding through them. It feels creepy seeing the foggy mass racing by right outside the window.

It's cloudy outside and people are hazy with fatigue and hangovers as they file off the plane. Sarah and I step out and look for the father, but we don't see him. We walk out into the hallway and people are walking away. Still there is no father.

Several minutes pass and now there are fewer people, which should make it easier to spot him. We don't.

Pretty soon all of the passengers and all of the crew have left and the place is completely deserted except for Sarah and me. And there is no father to pick us up.

I purposely keep my voice optimistic. "Maybe he just forgot it was today."

A uniformed man comes up to us and asks if we're okay and this makes me wonder if we are.

"I'm calling my dad," Sarah tells him.

He nods and walks off.

Sarah remembers the father better than I do and she's not optimistic at all. She's tired and disappointed. She thumbs through her purse to find the father's phone number. There is a pay phone down the hall so we walk to it and Sarah puts the dime in the slot and dials.

From what I can tell, a sleepy father answers the phone.

"We're here," Sarah tells him with feigned politeness. She listens, says, "Okay" and something about a gate number and hangs up.

"He'll be here in a while," she reports.

My head is buzzing. It does that when it hasn't had any sleep. I'm hungry, too, but food is a faraway thought. Leaning against a huge window that looks out upon the expanse of airport apparatus, I ignore my body's demands.

I'm determined to keep my optimism, mentally and sometimes verbally countering the discouragement I can see on Sarah's face. He didn't come to get us. He will be here but he takes his time and we don't need to be in any hurry anyway except that I'm very tired.

A tall man with dark hair walks toward us. He's one of those men who refuses hair loss and tosses a tuft over that balding spot on top. It's still slightly wet so he must have decided to take a shower before coming to get us and maybe this is why it took so long. I recognize him immediately but he's changed. He's older, evidenced by the gray sideburns that weren't there when I saw him four and a half years ago. He's smiling, which is a good sign, but it still feels weird to see a character from my distant past. Despite my mental fatigue, I experience a bit of anxiety, wondering if I know him at all and if he is *really* the father.

Sarah seems only slightly happy to see him. Now I realize it's my turn to step up and be the good girl. I'm not focusing on the father's meanness. I'm just glad to be away from Hawaii.

There are no hugs and "oh, I've missed you and welcome to Portland, and, oh, we're going to have so much fun while you're here." That level of tenderness would make all of us extremely uncomfortable.

"How was your flight?" he asks as we make our way to Baggage Claim. "Did you see Mount Hood?"

"I saw a mountain out there. Is that what it's called?" I ask with my most interested intonation.

Sarah and I will quickly learn that the father is a huge fan of Mt. Hood and its ski slopes and all the fun he has with his friends, skiing by day, drinking by night. This is the kind of life you can have when your responsibilities are thousands of miles away, I guess.

I want to ask the father about Nellie. I haven't seen my long lost sister for four and half years and I wonder about her. But right now I'm too fatigued to bring her up.

The northwest air has a bite and I'm hoping that the car is close. The father carries our suitcase and leads us to a sports car with a yellow curvy body and a black top. Somehow it seems appropriate for his world. There isn't much room in the backseat but I squeeze in.

"I don't live very far from the airport, you know, and that's why I just waited for you to call."

Sarah is quiet. Despite my weariness, I make an effort to keep the dialog going. "So, how big is Portland?"

"It's just the right size. There's a lot to do but it's not as big as the other major cities. It's easy to get around. So where's your tan?"

This question completely blindsides me. "What?" I ask, looking at Sarah.

"I had expected you two to come back with a dark Hawaiian tan but you don't look like you've been in the sun."

What? I ask again, but not out loud. He disapproves of me already. Why the hell didn't I get a tan before coming here? I'm an idiot.

"It's different when you *live* there."

I hear Sarah in the front seat agreeing with me as my mind catapults me back to touristy Kona with its chaise lounges and crystal pools. Maybe I should elaborate, but the words are stuck in my throat.

***

"Good God, you guys bring enough stuff?"

When the father says "good God," I bristle. He's mad even though he's sort of smiling, like it was a rhetorical question. Or was it?

Our suitcase is opened up on the floor of the father's living room. He sees everything we piled in to it and I can tell this concerns him. Perhaps he's got the idea that this is a short visit and that we'll be going back to the mother and stepfather, but there is no way in hell I'm going back there and I know Sarah feels the same way.

The father suggests we get some sleep. He grabs his keys and heads out the door before I can muster the nerve to say that it's been almost twenty-four hours since Sarah and I have eaten anything.

I wake to snippets of "Billy Don't Be a Hero." Music. A good omen.

It's early afternoon. I've been asleep on the floor of the father's tiny apartment. Sarah is next to me, still asleep. I pop my head up to see where the music is coming from. The father's sliding glass door is open and the sun is shining. Another good omen. The music is coming from one of the other apartments.

Sitting up, I can see the father's hi-fi against the wall. It looks exactly the same as it did all those years ago at the house on Hollis Street and the house at Echo Bend. I wonder if he'll let me touch it *now*.

My head is still buzzing. I haven't slept long enough but it will have to suffice. I can hear feet slapping the concrete steps outside. He's back. This rouses Sarah. The father walks in and we meet the first of his many lady friends.

"Girls, this is Dena."

Sarah sits up and yawns while Dena sits down on the father's bachelor style sofa. It's made of a low pile brown fur that begs to be petted like a friendly cat.

I sit on the floor in my halter dress. It's wrinkled now. I still haven't eaten anything since lunch yesterday, but I'm more tired than hungry.

"What a cute dress," Dena says and I like her. "Where's your tan?" and I don't like her.

"It's different when you *live* in Hawaii," I reply and mentally kick myself a second time for not getting a tan before coming here. But at least my response was quicker this time.

Dena lives in the apartment complex, downstairs in an adjacent building, just past the swimming pool. Her boyfriend is Rick and he has two daughters around our ages, we're informed.

"We'll all get along great together," Dena says enthusiastically as if she's aware that her words are exactly what I need to hear right now.

Rick and the father are friends but Dena likes the father, too, and he likes her and they spend a lot of time at her apartment.

Two more times I hear the dreaded, "Where's your tan?" after the father introduces us to more of his friends. I suppose they're just making friendly conversation but they don't know my history and how easy it is for adults to hurt my feelings.

More than anything I'm mad at myself for not leaving Hawaii with a tan so these people would stop doubting me. Yes, that's it. It's like they don't *really* think I came from Hawaii because if I did, I would be prancing around with golden skin, showing off, "Hey, everybody look at me, I came from Hawaii, aren't I something?" which is total hooey. Coming from Hawaii is nothing to advertise. At least not the Hawaii I came from.

While the father is at work, Sarah and I spend our summer beside the pool, working on those elusive tans while obsessing over "American Top 40."

***

Rick and his daughters and all of us drive to Kah-Nee-Ta in central Oregon. There is a large pool—and lifeguards! I swear one of them is watching me with interest. I'm watching him, too. He's seated up there on his chair and he's cute and he's got *a tan*. Baking in the sun, I start to fantasize about having a boyfriend and how cool it would be until my inner critic reminds me that I'm not cute enough to be liked by any guy and he's probably looking at some older girl sunning herself somewhere over there. I look behind me to see who she is; she could be a hundred people.

Walking into the bathroom, I look in the mirror at my shoulders and they're dark brown. *My God, I'm tanned.*

Despite the tan, school is disaster. Nobody cares whether I have a tan or not. I don't fit in. I can't make friends. I'm scared of doing things wrong. I have a painful history of doing things wrong and looking wrong and being wrong. I take out my anger on the pages of my journal, now an eight by ten binder filled with notebook paper.

Crystal is tall, thin, and model perfect. Her eyes are marquise cut and chestnut like her hair. She turns heads. She's also got insidious radar for the malleable. I'm both ignorant and flabbergasted that someone so pretty would have anything to do with me. We become friends before I see her true colors. She's controlling and manipulative. She causes me to second guess myself. For instance, when I ask her for my hairbrush.

"It's in my locker," she says and walks off in a huff.

I'm a fish out of water, flopping around, learning everything the hard way. I had to learn the social rules of Hawaii and now it's these bewildering mainland rules. I'm stymied. I don't know how to make friends.

***

The father doesn't hit Sarah or me but his raised voice indicates that he really doesn't like his daughters living with him and soiling his home and messing with his solitary routine. I'm the good girl now. I've learned to be affable around him, listen attentively, act like what he says is important and *always* have a quick answer for his questions because I'll do anything to keep from going back to Hawaii. Anything.

Not so for Sarah. Her good girl tank has run dry. I think there is too much pain, too many years of abuse; the scars are tender to the touch and it seems that they're always being irritated by the moody father.

Sarah is here one day, gone the next—a runaway. I'm full of mixed feelings. We were constantly on each other's nerves, stuck inside the four walls of this tiny apartment, dealing with school and homework and teachers and classmates and the father. I'm glad she's gone and I'm mortified that I could be *glad* she's gone.

The father, coming to terms with our permanence, has made a concession of sorts. He's arranging legal custody of Sarah and me. With Sarah gone, I'll go before the judge by myself.

Driving to the courthouse, he tells me his reasons. "I don't want to get a bigger place and buy furniture and then have your mother make legal demands for you. I will have wasted all that money."

I don't really care what his reasons are. I'm just not ever going back to Hawaii. Ever. In fact, lately I've been having these weird feelings that if I ever did go back to Hawaii, I'd be trapped there and never be able to leave. It feels very real so I'm taking it seriously.

"So, do you want to live with your father?" the judge asks from behind his big desk, three walls of books surrounding him. His presence is imposing and powerful.

"Yes." I should say "Yes, Sir" or "Yes, Your Honor" but I don't know the rules, and he overlooks my ignorance.

"Okay, you can go back to your father."

The mother is here and although it's only been a few months since I last saw her, she's like a different person, a person from my past, a stranger. It feels like our time together was a dream, as if the entire cast of characters from my past never really existed. I just made them up, let them pass through, and forgot them.

The mother and I don't talk to each other, which is a tragedy I'm too young to comprehend. The father has been feeding me abject comments about her. I'm familiar with this since the mother used to feed me a similar poison. They hate each other. Their mutual disgust is palpable. However, the father's is more overt.

"Good God, what did she do to her hair? It's snow white," the father whispers to me, completely repulsed.

The custody decision is done in a matter of minutes, all civil and proper. I say a quick goodbye to the mother, feeling kind of sad and vindicated at the same time.

But I'm still so very depressed about Adam, and about Sarah. What was once a family is now a gigantic tragedy, shattered and scattered.

***

I really want to have a friend, so I devote myself to overlooking Crystal's controlling nature.

After school, we wander around, over to the grade school to shoot hoops—I always miss—and to the convenience store a few blocks away to harass this guy named Gary behind the counter. He's a ragtag ex-con-looking guy who gives the impression he's ready to commit his next crime. I bet he hides a butcher knife in his sock, but I tell myself he's harmless.

Fueled by deviousness and stupidity, Crystal and I start calling Gary and hanging up, or calling him and asking him questions—basically tormenting him. I keep expecting him to get angry, but apparently he enjoys the attention.

While Crystal is out of town, I call him and we talk for a while. He asks me if I want to go out and I say "Sure."

I'm waiting by the curb and up drives Gary behind the wheel of a run down, paint-and-muffler-deprived, exhaust-spitting four-on-the-floor.

"Where are we going?"

"My place. I've just been to a wedding, man."

He's telling me about how fun this wedding was and I'm listening as the pickup chugs up 102nd Avenue toward the Banfield Freeway. He veers to the right and heads down to join the speeding traffic. Doubts about my decision begin to rise.

At 82nd he signals and exits. He's going kind of fast, too fast to make the turn. The pickup slams into the support pillar.

It's over before I realize it happened. And once the reality jars my shell-shocked brain, auto pilot takes charge.

Somehow, I open the door, climb out and start walking back toward the freeway, retracing my steps. I need to get home, undo this stupid day and this stupid trip with this guy I don't even know.

For a split second, I imagine him stumbling out and surveying his damaged pickup, scratching his head and saying, "Whoa, man."

The cars, thousands of them, speed by me here where the freeway meets the off ramp. How can I get home? Where am I? There is no oxygen to fuel my brain despite the constant swoosh of traffic-air slamming into my face. My slow-moving brain is an ironic juxtaposition to the speeding traffic. Gradually, it dawns on me that I can't walk home along the freeway. I turn back on what feels more like a treadmill than asphalt. I'm moving, but I'm not going anywhere.

A car has stopped beside the crashed pickup. It must have passed me but I don't remember seeing it. The driver and his wife graciously offer us a lift.

Riding in the backseat, Gary takes my hand and holds it, crafting a sordid illusion of comfort and camaraderie for me as well as the front seat occupants. He wants to be legitimate. He wants *us* to be legitimate. I don't refuse him and yet I don't even know him.

An anxious, robotic "Don't tell my dad," is all I'm capable of vocalizing. I keep saying it over and over like a mentally ill person who is also deaf. Maybe I'm in shock, thinking about how angry the father will be when he finds out. That seems to be my only clarity at the moment: the father will shit bricks if he finds out about this.

"I'll call you," Gary says and they drive off. I walk upstairs, still dazed. The father isn't here. I hobble to the twin-sized mattress on the floor of his bedroom and fall on it. I want to die..

Lying here, mulling over my fucked up day, I think Gary must have been drunk, maybe a little too much champagne at the wedding reception, although he didn't really seem like a champagne kind of guy. He certainly wasn't dressed like one. Now I'm thinking he was more the case-of-beer or the fifth-of-Jack Daniels type.

I consider this cryptic, naïve need I have buried inside and how, out of desperation, it plucks its head up from the depths just long enough to mess me up.

Reaching for companionship is risky business. It's easy to get thwacked and spanked right back into reality, which just makes me want to retreat into nothingness. Gary calls but I tell him, "No, thanks."

I'm very stingy with second chances.

CHAPTER TEN

Heavy, pink curtains veil the tiny room and convey a feeling of complete seclusion. She sets the baby down and walks out. Now she's lying on a bed, arms resting above her head while a man sits over her and caresses her breasts. Her eyes are closed and she's moaning. Then she's looking out the window at the mailbox by the street, wondering if the baby is awake inside the mailbox or if it's even in the mailbox anymore. She thinks she should go out and look.

I wake up.

The mother sends letters that tell of her generic goings on. Golf games, travel plans, volcano activity. Her dispassionate reporting on the mean grandma and the scary aunt and the scary uncle and how the weather's been leaves little room for Adam and this disappoints me, but it's just how she is, I remind myself. Then she signs the letters, *Love, Mom.* For my birthday she sends me a card, signed *Love, Mom, Boyd & Adam.* There is a check and I get it cashed and buy myself something nice.

I'm fourteen now. Sarah is still gone. I haven't heard from her for over a month and I'm not sure anyone else cares enough to look for her.

"Mom invited me to fly home for Christmas," I tell the father.

He sits on the sofa, briefcase open, important papers peeking out. Absentmindedly, he says, "It's up to you."

How stupid does a bird have to be to fly back inside its cage? And not just any cage, but a cage full of monsters with steely daggers poking it and tormenting it by day and by night. I'd have to be a complete moron to go back there. The mother is either oblivious to how much I hate Hawaii, or else she feels guilty. I've been *warned* not to go back. Hawaii is in my past and that's where it's staying.

***

Thanks to another overly dramatic begging and pleading episode, I agree to tag along with Crystal to her cousins' house. Big mistake. The adults are drinking upstairs where it's warm. Children are sequestered in the basement, painfully lacking entertainment or an adequate heat source.

It's getting late and I'd like to get home but, like an idiot, I went well beyond the call of duty, conceding to Crystal's overnight invitation. At three a.m., even the floor of her bedroom would be better than here in this strange, icy house.

Crystal's father is in no condition to drive. As we walk out to the car, the chill of winter is no match for his swagger and loose tongue—telltale signs of drunkenness. I should know, having seen similar behavior with

Gary not that long ago. After that nightmare, I'm worried about being in the car with another drunk but I see no other option.

Despite the fact that it's late and I should be sleepy, I'm wide awake, probably because I keep having visions of going off the road while simultaneously thinking of ways to get out of the car, but all roads lead to Crystal's father. I'd have to actually *talk* to him. No way. He's menacing and loud and has a temper. He wears cowboy boots and he spits.

Crystal is oblivious to the peril surrounding us, evidenced by her uncharacteristic muteness and sagging eyelids, barely visible in the darkness. I'm sure my life is going to end tonight.

If I *do* survive, I tell myself, if by some sheer undeserved miracle I make it back to Crystal's house in one piece, without any blood or guts, I promise I'll never, *ever* be caught again in a vehicle with Crystal's dad. He's fucking crazy.

***

Government Camp is a modest Oregon town-let situated at the 3,800 foot level on the southern flanks of Mt. Hood. It's a rustic place with chunky wooden pubs, crude diners, and a viable general store hugging the main street. Clusters of winter cabins dot the outskirts under a hovering cloud of wood smoke. During a good winter, several feet of snow blanket the area and muffle the traffic noise on the nearby highway. Government Camp's close proximity to the ski slopes affords die-hard skiers—such as the father—a convenient nighttime respite.

Although I relish my weekends alone at the father's apartment, skiing holds a certain fascination as well. I decide to give it a try.

A historic rope tow disaster sends missives of caution to keep me cognizant of my accident-prone nature. I must have been four or five years old, desperate to follow in the footsteps of my older sisters, Nellie and Sarah, who were already proficient at the fine art of downhill skiing.

"When you grab onto the rope tow, do it *gently*," Sarah warned.

I was unable to comprehend *gently* and quickly toppled over into a leg-wrenching heap that landed me in the first aid center. For weeks, I hobbled around with a painful, swollen knee.

Now, though, I find the chairlift is more doable than a rope tow. After twice bringing it to an abrupt halt—once while trying to embark and falling and again while trying to disembark and falling—I gather my wits, dust off my humiliation, and feign expertise for just a second before falling again.

A cloud of steam emanates from the father's heavy sigh and reveals his plethora of doubts about my downhill abilities. He's obviously embarrassed by the total klutziness of his offspring. He gazes up at his buddies running the ski lift and rolls his eyes. They nod back a smirking, "I pity you, dude."

Adjusting his goggles and grabbing his poles, he says, "Watch me" and glides effortlessly down the slope. He stops in a fanciful showoff maneuver, turns and looks back up at my sorry form and yells, "Now go."

I go, pushing with my poles. He yells, "Traverse," and I spread the skis and shift my weight but I end up in a heap. My bindings release and now I've got to find a way to get my boot back into a buried ski while encased in an overly puffy ski "parka", as the father calls it.

For the father's critical eye, I scramble up quickly. He's got to see that I'm trying and that his efforts aren't in vain. Still, completely exasperated, he turns away and swoops and swooshes down the hill and out of sight.

I swallow and exhale my own puff of steam and rid myself of that brief image of him side-stepping back up the hill to help me. I unceremoniously plop my padded butt onto the snow. I must figure things out for myself.

What feels like hours later, I make it to the bottom of what I finally realize is a hill much too steep for a beginner. The lodge beckons.

When the father supplies me with shorter skis, the whole process becomes a lot easier. Having already mastered every mistake known to man, I can finally understand the allure and I don't feel like a complete imbecile any longer, at least not on the slopes. It's a pleasant feeling to be good at something.

When it gets dark, we head back to Government Camp and the cabin the father shares with several of his friends.

A sizeable group of adults has just departed on their evening pilgrimage to the Ratskeller. It's quiet. The cabin is cozy, half-buried in winter snow. Before they left, one of the men set up a nice fire in the massive rock fireplace implanted along the outer wall of the living room.

Phil and I are the only ones here now. He's a few years older but has lived a pretty sheltered life, I can tell. I think it's time for him to live it up a little. Besides, that bottle of wine on the kitchen counter has been calling and it's time to answer.

I grab some glasses, pour, and hand Phil his portion, saying, "Bottoms up." I guzzle round one. We walk toward the living room but there is no point in sitting down with an empty glass. I turn around and head back to the kitchen which is, conveniently, only a few steps away.

Phil is tentative, sipping slowly and watching me. It's going to take him forever to get looped. Never mind. I'm already working on round two. I saunter back, plop myself on the sofa, a little too close. Phil's probably getting the wrong idea, but I don't care.

"Oops." I spilled a little bit on the carpet and this makes me giggle. Phil's trying to tell me something but I'm drinking and wiping wine off my chin.

Words pop out of his mouth and sink into a pool of drone.

He's sort of getting closer, moving in. But he's a neophyte. I might be, too, but I won't admit it because the wine is gifting me with a blissful superiority, coupled with a cavalier "who gives a shit" attitude.

My glass is empty. I stand up too fast and feel bit woozy as I turn toward the kitchen.

I can tell Phil's confidence is draining as fast as my wine glass. He's getting paranoid. Suddenly he's become aware that I'm more interested in making love to the drink than to him.

Another round for me, a shallow refill for Phil. Sadly, he's not really having very much fun except for every now and then he'll let out a little laugh at something I say. I lean forward and, even though Phil is older than me, I feign motherliness and pat Phil's knee and tell him, "Thop worryeering" between uncontrollable giggles, and "Dreenk uph!"

But he still drinks slowly and watches me as I keep lumbering back to the bottle on the counter, pouring more, spilling it, and sloshing it into my mouth, breaking into another uncontrollable giggle. "Oops, all gonne. Thime for a reefill," as I stagger back toward that magnetic bottle for yet another round.

He keeps saying, "I think you've had enough," and he comes and stands between me and the bottle.

And I keep slurring, "Nonnthense" and pushing him aside and stumbling and giggling.

Time is irrelevant but the gallon is nearing empty and the fire has ebbed to embers. The sound of muffled chatter and boots stomping off snow are harbingers of the adults' dreaded return. I swagger my way to my little partitioned sleep area and my spinning head hits the pillow and continues to spin into oblivion.

***

The view from the lodge's window seat is pleasant enough. Clusters of pointy conifers border thick white strips sprinkled with tiny ants zigzagging down the hill. The view would include me if I wasn't so nauseous. The headache I've been nursing all morning is nearing the migraine stage and the smell of food isn't helping. The hangover is part of the deal, the penalty for overindulgence, like a parent sending the kid to his bedroom to "think about what you've done." But I'm too miserable to think.

***

"It's easy to rip off things," Crystal proclaims totally out of the blue one day. "You just tuck something into your hand and walk away and then slip it into your pocket or your purse. Easy."

So far so good. I've gotten small things like lipstick and eye liner and I'm feeling downright smug about my new-found malfeasance.

We're halfway to the neighborhood variety store when I realize I've forgotten the key to my bike lock. I yell up to Crystal, leading the way which is her assumed role in all our endeavors—her leading, me following. "I left my bike lock at home."

"So what?" she snarls. "It's not worth going all the way back. We'll just park our bikes right by the door and they'll be okay."

Having tentatively assumed Crystal's resoluteness, I park my bike alongside hers and we walk inside the store, taking our chances with unlocked bikes.

Within five or so minutes, a lady comes up to me and it's like she knows me, but for the life of me, I can't place her. "Did you leave your bike parked outside?" she asks.

"Yes." I'm bewildered.

"Well, it just got stolen."

Crystal is within earshot and a young kid she knows is repeating the woman's words. The two of them walk over to us. Crystal wears an indiscernible countenance.

"Some guys just rode off on them," the woman continues.

Crystal and I walk outside. and, sure enough, the bikes are gone. It feels like someone just ripped out my heart. I don't have the capacity to assimilate my feelings because my head is stuck inside some kind of cold tomb, disconnected from my body.

After the policeman scribbles stuff on his note pad, he offers us a ride home. Having lost my enthusiasm for shoplifting, I accept.

I ride, staring out the window. As the blood slowly returns to my brain, I can't help but deliberate on the sheer irony of it: riding in a police car, not because I got busted but because I'm the victim.

Alone at the father's apartment, I'm free to think, allow the reality to sink in. My beloved bike was *stolen*. The many hours I labored, babysitting to earn enough money to buy it, and the freedom it provided. Now it's in the hands of some stranger who is oblivious to my connection to it. This feeling of betrayal is sickening.

I will *never* rip off another thing from a store, ever. This whole situation feels like a lesson from something bigger than me. I can't ignore it. I don't know if God does stuff like this, but maybe He does and I think I'd better listen if it *is* God warning me—and I think it is.

Crystal believes in God. She even goes to a Catholic church, so she'll understand and agree with my decision. And she does. For about two days.

Riding the city bus to Lloyd Center Mall, I purposely don't say a lot. I'm steadfast in my resolve. No shoplifting. Crystal is fickle. There is a purse she needs to have.

"Go ahead if you want, but I'm not stealing anything," I say.

She mistakes my stance for snubbing. Maybe I am a little overly confident, but I'm unwavering. Nothing will change my mind.

"You're chicken."

I'm silent. I've already crossed the line and pissed her off. I'm just going to sit here silently with my personal ruling.

The store is almost uncomfortably warm. I could take my coat off but I'd better not since it might arouse suspicion even though I'm innocent of any wrongdoing.

We've been browsing independently for several minutes. Crystal walks up to me. "Let's go."

"Okay."

At this point, I can't tell whether she lifted this got-to-have purse or not. I'm empty-handed except for the purse I brought with me.

Stepping into the mall area, someone comes up behind us, grabs our arms and says, "Excuse me, but you'll need to come with me."

Oh. shit.

"You can sit there." A rather buff and tough-looking person, presumably a female, has escorted us down a flight of stairs to this tiny, windowless office. Intimidation. Her counterpart walks in, sits down behind a desk. and the aforementioned escort stands beside her.

"We'd like to see your belongings."

"Okay," I toss my purse on the desk and Crystal folds her arms. She's indignant, thinking she can still get away with this if she plays her cards right. I'm all for getting the whole thing over with and getting the hell out of here.

"So what did you take?" the woman asks looking straight at Crystal, handing my purse back to me.

She's silent, arms folded, hoity-toity written all over her face. She's *better* than this.

"Just tell them," I whisper, then louder, "She's got it inside her jacket." Why it doesn't occur to me to keep my mouth shut, I haven't a clue. I guess I'm only thinking about myself and my anxiety and my prearranged innocence and Crystal's universal stupidity. I just want to get the hell out of this creepy, godforsaken pseudo-jail and away from these menacing men/women. Besides, it's not like we weren't *warned*. But I don't tell Crystal this because she's already fuming.

She opens her coat and throws the purse in question onto the desk with a loud huff that says, "I'm not sorry I stole it, I'm just sorry I got caught."

"Thank you. From now on you are not welcome in this store. Do I make myself clear?"

Crystal continues to sit with her arms folded but she's reluctantly nodding.

"You can leave now and I don't ever want to see you in this store again," she repeats, like we need to hear it one more time. Whether this policy includes me or not, I couldn't say since getting the hell out of here is my solitary ambition.

***

Laying on my mattress on the floor of the father's bedroom, the ceiling becomes my movie screen as I replay this freaky day. I'm beginning to wonder if God—whoever He is—is watching me and keeping me from screwing up my life any more than it already is. In some nebulous metaphysical way, these scattered wonderings are coalescing into something remotely resembling faith. Maybe it *is* God and maybe I can pray and He's going to hear me. Maybe if I just follow the commandments, like *don't steal*, He'll help me.

Rising from the mattress, I tiptoe over to the father's bedroom window. I can see the airplanes if I look to the left and watch the distant sky. Actually, the airplanes aren't all that distant and sometimes they're pretty close. I guess it depends on which runway they're planning to land on. I'd kind of like to learn more about these ominous, enigmatic machines that chauffeur people all over the planet and defy the laws of gravity. I'm terrified of being a passenger, but they also intrigue me.

Tonight is one of those nights when the pilots are opting for the closer runway. Cool. It's twilight and just a smidgen of daylight remains in the western sky. An airplane is inching its way closer to Earth, drifting peacefully like a swan on a lake. The lights are on—all of the tiny window lights, lined up and stretching from the front of the plane clear to the back, and all of the twinkling lights on the wings, the upturned tail end, the front nose end, and the belly. It looks peaceful and serene out there twinkling away as it leaves my sight. I wonder, are the passengers as peaceful, or are they a bundle of nerves like I was?

I absentmindedly look down. From this second story vantage point, it's easy to see the traffic coming and going along Prescott Avenue.

A red Charger-type car thunders down the otherwise placid twenty-five-mile-an-hour zone. It's losing control. It crosses the center lane, fishtails, and slams into a sign pole. And all of this happened right in front of me, in about three seconds.

When I open my eyes, it won't be there. But it's there, a stone's throw away from the father's upstairs window. Looking down at the fizzling, rumpled heap, I can see two blonde headed children in the backseat.

Floating toward the kitchen, the father's wine has never looked more enticing. With siren sounds getting louder, I set the glass down and succumb to morbid curiosity. People have gathered, but this is all I can see due to the visceral agony choking me.

I top off the glass, swallow, and walk into the living room. The lights are off and I can see the emergency lights flickering around and around against the father's darkened living room walls.

I push the gray button on the father's stereo. A jazz song from the father's KINK radio station is playing. I turn the knob to KISN but remind myself to be sure to turn it back to KINK before I turn it off. It's important to take every available precaution to keep from pissing off the father. He finds enough to get pissed off about without my help.

I change my mind and start up *Band on the Run*. I need new music. This album is starting to wear on me and it reminds me too much of the life I left behind; a life I'm forbidden to think about. But, still, I like "Bluebird" and when I see the Bluebird sign on the school buses parked across the street, I'm reminded of this song and Hawaii and that elusive rescuer that I ended up not needing after all. The whole thing is so preposterous, I tell myself. Yet if I dig any deeper into my memory bank, I get a stabbing pain in my chest and down my arm. It hurts—literally.

The father is out on a date. He's got so many women I can't keep them straight. He'll date one for a while and I'll think, okay, she's nice. I'll get used to her and then he'll drop her and the whole thing will start over. It's starting to make me go numb and I'm thinking that I just won't care anymore. It's not like he's getting married. I'm polite, but I'm getting cynical.

At least his love life is better than mine. I like these foxy guys but I'm too afraid to talk to them and I'm sure they'd think I was a nobody if they even knew I existed.

***

Sam has been walking home from school with me for a few weeks now. He lives nearby in a big, brick house. His room is upstairs and sometimes when Crystal and I walk by, he waves from his window.

He asks me, "What are you doing this afternoon?"

I say, "Nothing."

We say goodbye at the street corner. He tells me, "I'd walk the rest of the way, but I don't know what to do when we get to the door."

I lamely respond with, "I don't know, either," and I don't let myself think about how weird this is.

He walks home with me for several more days and says goodbye at the street corner.

And now he's walking all the way to the father's apartment building and he asks what I'm doing this afternoon.

"Nothing." I say goodbye and he says goodbye and he goes on his way.

And pretty soon he's walking right to the bottom of the stairs. He's showing me the chocolate bar he wants to share. I'm thinking, okay, no biggie. I'm not really thinking about why he wants to come in and I'm not thinking "no" because I don't know how to say no. I don't know what's coming. Nobody warned me about this kind of guy.

He sits on the brown sofa and we talk about nothing while he breaks apart the candy bar and hands me a piece like I'm interested. I take it from him because I can't say "no." I'm just taking it to be polite.

When the chocolate is gone, he tells me he wants to do it.

What? It takes a few minutes to line up his words into something comprehensible.

So he says it several times. I've got it now but I still don't really get it.

He's talking about sex on the twin sized mattress on the floor in the father's bedroom, the place where I sleep.

Once it all officially sinks in, I tell him, "No way." And I should tell him to get the fuck out of my house, but I don't.

He ignores my reply and repeats himself. "Come on."

I'm repeating, "No. I don't want to," but my body is getting mysteriously heavy.

He's not stupid and he knows he's wearing me down. He's not being forceful or demanding or anything. He's just sitting here, telling me he wants to do it.

I'm powerless. I'm in a stupor, a bewildering aura of some kind. This whole thing just cannot be happening.

My body has mysteriously morphed into a statue, a leaden, inanimate object. Time stands still. He keeps telling me he wants to do it. He's not touching me or forcing me or anything.

I'm saying no a little quieter now, looking down at my feet, a twisted smile on my face, like I need to be polite, which I know on some level is complete insanity. I'm wishing he'd go but I can't tell him to get out of my house.

How long have we been here?

"Come on."

I've plummeted into some kind of nihilistic fugue. I've become nothing. There is no guard, no me, just this softened, permeable membrane, mumbling an unconvincing "no" in response to Sam's droning "Come on."

Why won't he leave? Because I haven't *told* him to leave. I can't make myself tell him to get out and leave me alone so I just look down with this twisted perma-smile.

Through the desert fog, encapsulated in the most infinitesimal time measurement, a thought speeds through my brain. "I could probably kick this guy's ass if I wanted to." But my brain can't hold the thought and it evaporates.

"Come on."

Silence.

"Okay." A whisper. I'm a little girl.

I can barely make eye contact with Sam, but I detect a victory smile that is supposed to portray something like kindness but doesn't. He grabs my hand and leads my leaden body to the bedroom where he unzips my pants and he unzips his and he tells me to lie down on my twin sized mattress and he lies down and squeezes himself inside me.

Like the chocolate dissolving in my mouth, my essence evaporates, consumed by an unwelcome intruder. I'm somewhere else, but I'm not. I'm here. I'm a blend of nothingness and utter shame, melting into a putrid pool on the mattress.

He gets up. "If you tell anyone what we did, I'll tell them you're a *whore*."

"Okay," I say, nodding pathetically. I'm a little girl, following orders.

He repeats himself, "If you tell anyone what we did, I'll tell them you're a whore."

"I won't tell." And from the depths of my core rises the tiniest inkling of pride. I refuse to verbalize that I don't know what a *whore* is.

He leaves. And this is how I lose my virginity. No amorous I love you promises, but he didn't stick a knife to my throat, either.

I let him. I wasn't stoned or drunk but I was mysteriously inebriated.

Later, when I have the mental clarity to think about it, the whole event will illuminate what has been a covert forgone conclusion for many years: my complete ineptitude with living.

Don't worry, Sam. No one will ever know about this.

CHAPTER ELEVEN

I can't do anything right. The kitchen floor is sticky, the pantry shelves are a mess, and I'm fat.

There is no way to predict when the father will blow up. I look for a pattern, precipitating factors of some kind, but they don't exist. Or, if they do, they sure as hell elude me. Maybe I'm not looking hard enough or in the right places.

His rage usually occurs when I'm least expecting it.

I didn't vacuum the carpet and there are crumbs under the table and, "Good God, look at you … you ate all the cookies. Good god, stop eating all the cookies and go on a goddamned diet." He keeps ranting about my obesity while I wonder why my weight is such a big deal to him.

I can't tell him that Crystal ate the cookies because Crystal—and all of my other acquaintances—are banned from entering the father's apartment.

"And, good God, your stomach looks like you're pregnant."

Wait. What? Oh, shit. That last rant sucked all the air out of the room. What the hell did he just say? Fighting the urge to look down at my enormous girth, I wait for his tirade to run its course.

I walk to the bathroom and jump on the scale. A hundred and fifteen pounds fully clothed. Yep, I'm obese. I tell myself the magic number is ninety-five, and I make a vow to lose twenty pounds by summer.

But his "pregnant" comment haunts me. I look down and rub my flab and wonder if this is what pregnant looks like.

Sam didn't use a condom and my periods are erratic, occurring about once every four months. Before the father made that comment I hadn't even considered the possibility that I could be pregnant.

I just won't think about it. I can't think about it.

***

It's early morning and cloudy but by ten or eleven the clouds will burn off and the rest of the day will be sunny. This is the typical pattern for much of the summer in Portland.

I walk up the steps and ring the doorbell. An attractive divorcee answers and invites me in. She ushers me to the sofa and tells me her son, Robbie, is still asleep so I may as well make myself comfortable until he gets up, and that she'll be leaving in a few minutes.

Once she's gone, I get up and turn on the stereo, walk to Robbie's room to make sure he's okay, then go back to the sofa. It's still early, so I might as well catch a little nap before he wakes up.

Curling up in a throw blanket, I begin to drift off, thinking about my recent trip to visit Nellie in southern Oregon. It was good to get away from Crystal-the-control-freak for a while and see my sister.

Nellie and her husband are big time stoners. They grow and sell pot. And they smoke a hell of a lot of it, too. It doesn't seem to bother them, which I find baffling. After the first few days of being wasted, I couldn't shake the awful feeling that something terrible was going to happen, some catastrophic fire was going to burn me up or the car was going to crash and chew me to bits. It was freaky. I finally decided to stop so I could keep my sanity. But that makes me feel like a failure. Cool people get high. I hate the idea that I can't be cool because I can't smoke pot.

While I was at Nellie's, I started my period, so at least I know I'm not pregnant. Her kids are great, but I'm not ready to be a mom yet, and I sure don't need any reminders about my stupidity with Sam. What possessed me to allow such an embarrassing thing to happen? I hate Sam. If I could kill him and get away with it, I would.

***

Lying on the sofa, the scratchy afghan covering me, I can't hear the stereo. I know I turned it on. I'm asleep but I'm awake, too. Aren't I? My body is buzzing and shaking in a way I've never experienced. It's terrifying, like electricity seizing my entire being. No, it's an entity, something evil. I want to move but I can't. I know I'm asleep on the sofa but I can't wake up. I can't open my eyes and my whole body is paralyzed and fighting against itself.

Out the window, a man walks by. Dark hair, mustache, white lab coat, walking toward the trailer door. *Panic.* I need to get up and make sure the door is locked… I don't want that man coming in here … and he is!

I'm in a state of crisis. I'm trying wake myself up. I'm on the sofa, but I'm not. I'm in a trailer … I can't wake up and I can't hear the stereo and I can't open my eyes and I can't move. I've got to check the lock on the door because this dream might be a warning. Maybe the man with the dark hair and the mustache and the lab coat, maybe he's *really* outside trying to get in.

Finally, after wrestling with the eerie, creepy, completely *freaky* dream—or whatever it was—I somehow free myself and become fully conscious.

I rise and open the blinds. The clouds are already burning off and warm sunlight fills the room. I glance over at that sofa and although it looks normal now, I know I just underwent some bizarre demonic visitation in that spot. There must be something like electricity there or a gateway to an alternate reality, a portal to a dark, evil place. I'm still dazed and freaked out by it. I'll just stay away from that couch and sit on the chair or something, I decide, shivering.

I walk to the kitchen, grab a piece of paper and a pen, and write down everything that just happened. Then I fold the paper and put it in my purse.

Robbie walks out and his voice reminds me that I'm not alone here in this scary house. There is breakfast to make and everything else to do. I'm forced to switch gears, which is a good thing because it means I can get my mind off of all that bizarre stuff, at least for now. And as I bustle around, I'm strangely comforted by the folded piece of paper tucked inside my purse.

***

The woman disrobes and heads toward the waves. It's late and dark and any moron would know that swimming with sharks is pure folly, but she doesn't suspect anything and dives in and heads out and—wham—something takes her leg off and then it circles around and comes back for the other. She screams but no one hears her. Blood fills the water. She screams again, then gets jerked under the surface, and we no longer hear her screams. She's gone. In the morning, what's left of her body washes ashore and the passerby who finds it is grossed out and shocked and calls the authorities. And so goes the *Jaws* saga, or at least how I remember it, a creature so menacing and hungry it would actually jump aboard a ship and *eat* the human occupants with a very 70's full bass rhythmicity.

Over the summer, I decided I wanted to be bookish. Before seeing *Jaws* in the theater, I would immerse myself in the happenings on Amity Island. Peter Benchley's words mesmerized me as I cultivated my secret crush on Police Chief Martin Brody. He was a dashing hero who would stop at nothing, including risking his own life, to save his people who were heavily enmeshed in shark terror.

The crush didn't come from seeing him on screen If anything, I was a little shy and embarrassed when I saw him in action—a real man, not just someone I conjured up. No, it was reading about him all those weeks that fashioned the fantasy. I decided I *wanted* Police Chief Martin Brody because he overrides his fear of the water and rescues people. For some reason, I'm heavily drawn to the strong rescuer type.

***

The members of the father's social circle are a fairly predictable bunch. Collectively perched on the downward side of the hill, they camouflage their senescence by staying hip and cool, keeping it real, wearing leather. Maybe this attitude is what shapes their dreaded questions.

"Do you have a boyfriend?" they all ask.

It's not so much the question as the answer that pisses me off. Refusing eye contact, I mutter a sheepish, semi-apologetic "No." I could lie but I lack enough confidence to pull it off. "Yeah, I've been making out with David Cassidy." Or better yet, "I'm carrying David Cassidy's baby." That would teach them.

In response to my predictable answer, Rachel, whose husband Dave is the father's best friend, always pats my hand and says, "You have lots of time," in a very motherly tone. I want to like her but something indefinable holds me in check.

Can't she think of anything else to ask me? It used to be "Where's your tan?" Now it's "Do you have a boyfriend?" Why can't they ask me hip questions like "Have you seen *Jaws* yet?" Or even "How's your babysitting job going?" Something that doesn't cut right to the bone and reinforce my dismal existence.

I find it kind of mysterious, the father's esoteric world and his party friends. In a way I envy them because they're all cool and not just any cool but *very* cool. Bonnie Raitt cool. I don't really care what they're doing and yet, I'd like some of their *cool* to rub off on me.

***

Oddly, I've been getting really lonely for Sarah. I've been praying like crazy that I'll hear something, because she's been missing for so long. I'm worried that she's okay.

I've got a wallet sized photo of her. "Now, you call me, you hear?" I tell her. I'm sure she can't hear me but maybe God can and maybe he'll nudge her or something. Maybe God can do that for me, if he does this kind of thing. I haven't ripped off anything since I made that promise, so maybe I'm on God's good side. And maybe he'll answer this prayer. If he does, I want to be here to answer the phone. Oh, and I'll have to pray that it's *not* Crystal on the other end.

I plod over to the sofa for a few minutes of shut-eye. I'm depressed.

The phone's ring abruptly terminates my nap.

"Hello?"

"Hi, there."

It's Sarah! I can hardly believe my ears. It was what, like, fifteen minutes ago I was praying to God and now she's calling after a year of silence.

***

Sarah is seated across from me in this icy Formica booth. We agreed to meet at this restaurant because she didn't want a chance meeting with the father.

She and Brenda are both completely shit-faced. They're loud and rowdy. I stifle a laugh so I won't add to the ruckus and instinctively look over at the people seated at a booth near the door. I'm a little bit embarrassed.

Sarah refuses to answer my surplus of questions and steers me away from all things serious. She doesn't actually say "lighten up." She just disguises her answers with laughter and inside jokes with Brenda. Their antics are pretty entertaining, actually, and I suppose I *should* lighten up, laugh at their craziness.

And it's pretty obvious that the sacredness of her phone call approximately fifteen minutes after my fervent prayer would be completely sullied if I were to voice it under these circumstances.

After this chaotic exchange and insufficient reconnection, Sarah and Brenda declare their need to get going. They've got to catch their bus. We promise to meet again.

I ride my new bike back to the father's apartment and I'm feeling something, I'm not sure what.

I turn on the TV, and there is that Pepsi commercial that never fails to overwhelm me with sadness and remorse. It's Adam on screen, the little blond-headed boy. He's outside, sitting on the grass, and a bunch of happy puppies are jumping and licking him and he's laughing and laughing. It's a little boy laugh, genuine, complete, and contagious. It cuts deep into my soul and I bleed. It hurts worse than anything in the entire world. I miss Adam and I'm so sorry for how I treated him. I was so angry. What if I inflicted so much damage that he never is completely okay?

And the only way I can see my brother is if I go back to Hawaii, which I will *never* do.

CHAPTER TWELVE

Jayne's home is the antithesis of the father's apartment: big and spacious. It's situated in a calm, well-kept neighborhood on the eastern outskirts of Portland but still within the bounds of easy access to the bus lines.

How cool, finally having my own room. I can decorate how I want, mess things up or keep things picked up and not have anyone else's shit to deal with. I'd like to buy some posters for the walls and maybe even a stereo if I can save enough money. I'm hopeful that I can put my signature all over this room and feel like I've got a place in the world that's all mine. Maybe it's only because that sense of home has been missing for so long that I wish for it more fervently.

The father and Jayne are in love. Combining households is how love is consummated these days. They're in the garage, organizing a yard sale to get rid of the father's stuff while I'm carting the last of my boxes up to my room.

My bedroom—it still feels weird to call it that—is the first one at the top of the stairs. Keith and Justin, Jayne's two boys, must now share the corner room. Jayne's decorating prowess is evident everywhere and the boys' space is no exception. They've got cool wall beds that meet up at a sizable corner table. On the opposite wall is a large, long desk with "Puma" stamped all over. I'm not sure what that means. Shelves above the desk hold typical guy things like baseball photos and model airplanes that give off an air of permanence I can't comprehend. Sandwiched between the shelves is the ubiquitous Farrah Fawcett poster; she makes every other female on the planet look like a dog. I check to make sure no one is watching and then I stick out my tongue, scowl, and give her the finger.

The rest of the house is equally enchanting. There's a wet bar downstairs in the family room. It doesn't take long for my radar to home in on the contents behind the cabinet doors. Not just wine but *hard liquor*. I'm thinking that Jayne probably doesn't keep tabs on the fullness of the bottles and it will probably be easy to slip down here every now and then—like say, every night—for a nightcap. No, I tell myself. I've got to play it cool.

At the opposite end of the room is a sliding glass door that leads out onto the lower portion of the backyard. Someone affiliated with *Sunset* magazine designed and installed the landscaping. There's a central fire pit with permanently installed wood benches and planter boxes. It looks very magazine-chic. Beyond the backyard is a fenced Douglas fir forest belonging to the Girl Scouts with the promise that it won't be developed anytime soon.

I would think that indulging in all of this upper middle class suburban living with its sundry perks and conveniences and luxuries would make the recipients content and happy, carefree, harmonious, and congenial like a fairy tale. But nothing could be further from the truth, at least in this household. Tragically, after our brief honeymoon period, when "benefit of the doubt" and courteousness were the rule, things quickly devolved to irritations, disappointments, and generalized bickering.

Admittedly, I wear a myopic lens of skepticism. It magnifies the warts of disharmony and perches them at the seat of salience. Even though I'm only fifteen, I've become adept at watching and interpreting what I see. My observations may not be accurate, but they're all I've got to go by and I need them for survival.

The first red flag comes from Keith and Justin. I have a feeling they're not happy about my barging in and interrupting their routine. Keith was nice at first but it didn't take long for his arrogance to manifest. He's thirteen, crossing that threshold into the teen years. Even under the best of circumstances, I realize, this can be a dicey time. It's got to be so much worse with an alien person in the next room and an alien "father" to divert the mother's attentions and affections.

But I've got no tolerance for arrogance. Keith pushes my buttons and I shove his and it goes back and forth and, voila, I've got a new nemesis and he lives under the same roof—*his* roof and *I'm* the intruder, once again. I'm wondering if these four walls of my bedroom are up to the hefty task of keeping the world out.

Justin is eight and still encapsulated within the era of innocence. He's cute and sweet, the way kids naturally are when they still see the world though naïve simplicity. He bears a striking resemblance to his beautiful mother.

With my history, I ought to be a master at adapting to different living situations and different people with the moods and temperaments and all that goes with them. I'm not exactly sure what I'm doing wrong. Maybe it's that I crave alone time so much and the rest of the family interprets this as me being snobbish.

Despite my idiosyncrasies, Jayne makes what appears to be a genuine effort to connect with me.

"Would you like to go and get your hair cut and styled?"

I run my fingers through my hair. It is pretty ugly. I'm sure Jayne wants to make some improvements. And so I agree.

She treats me to a hair makeover at one of the trendiest, if not *the* trendiest salon in Portland. It probably costs a day's wages.

And then Jayne asks, "How about we go shopping at Nordstrom?"

Nordstrom? Is she out of her mind? The doorman would take one look at urchin-me and lock the door. But if I go with Jayne maybe he will make an exception, so I say "Sure." But I'm fat and none of the clothes will fit. I don't tell Jayne this.

She makes an appointment with an orthodontist. And I say "Sure" because it's blatantly apparent that I need a lot of improvements.

She's trying to connect with me and be motherly and do "girl things" but all I can see are my blaring failures and her attempts at trying to improve me. In response, I keep mentally bouncing from *What? Am I not good enough for you, ya prissy bitch?* to *God, I'm such scum, why is she even wasting her time with me?*

I can't figure out what's wrong with my thinking. Don't I want someone to care about me? Isn't Jayne kind of what I've wanted all along? A mother? An approachable female role model?

Maybe everything is so blurry because Jayne brings into focus what's been missing so long and my brain can't take it.

***

I've got a job to occupy my non-school hours. The day supervisor is training me on meat cooking. She walked off for a minute, leaving me to unwrap a twenty pound hunk of hamburger. I heave the bloody lump into a large rectangular commercial-grade frying pan and absentmindedly add the seasonings, just as I was told to do.

My mind is only half here. The other half is still trying to make sense of yet another freaky dream I had last night. This time it centered on murder and blood. I can't remember anything more than that but it left an indelible impression on my psyche. I feel like I'm in some sort of netherworld fog today. Robotically, I go about my restaurant tasks with just enough clarity to skim by.

Out of the blue, as I'm stirring the bloody hamburger, I see something. Some piece of my dream. "Oh, wow!"

"Are you okay?" asks the supervisor, with a puzzled look.

"Yeah. I just remembered something, but—" and I stop, shrug my shoulders and fake a weak smile. The supervisor walks away and I go back to mixing the simmering hamburger.

"What the hell was that?" I whisper to myself. I was flashing back to my dream and I saw something, but what? It felt vaguely familiar, like I was back in a place I know about, witnessing an event I know about, but I'll be damned if I can remember it now. The more I try, the more elusive it makes itself.

Lately I've had suspicions that I'm beginning to unravel. Just the other day I even wrote *I think I need to see a shrink* in my journal. And now, I *know* I'm losing it and the thought scares the shit out of me. I've got to get a grip, and fast.

CHAPTER THIRTEEN

I'm standing in line behind a tall partition. It's stuffy and warm and I'm nervous. My stomach is working overtime, lurching and wrestling with a bad case of the jitters. Ahead, steps lead up to a velvet curtain. As the queue inches closer to them, I keep replaying the scenario in my head, just like we rehearsed it.

It all started when Jayne arranged for me to get my hair cut at the aforementioned trendy salon. The beautician/owner thought my hair turned out so well that she called her partner/husband over and he looked at it and the two of them engaged themselves in a few moments of beautician-speak about angles and lines. I was sitting there feeling like an inanimate object, painted smile plastered on my lips that probably looked as fake as it felt, but they weren't looking at my face. Then he agreed with her that things looked satisfactory. Then she grabbed her camera and started snapping photos as she told me about this hair fashion show they were planning. And here I am. It's kind of an honor really. I mean, how many people get to be part of a fashion show?

"Are you nervous?"

I turn to the voice beside me and smile.

"Yeah, I just hope I don't trip or something. I'm most nervous about the fact that I'm a total klutz."

She laughs. She's a little bit younger than I am and she's wearing taffeta. Her hair is perfect. She's wearing a bit of make-up on her cheeks that looks wrong. Under the circumstances, I remind myself, it's perfectly acceptable.

I'm wearing a denim overall skirt with a white, long sleeved cotton shirt underneath. They belong to Jayne and I had to beg her to let me borrow them. She was reluctant, maybe because she thought I was too fat, but, surprisingly, they fit fine.

"I'm nervous, too," the girl says. I try to force a smile and keep the conversation alive but my manic mind and dry throat keep killing it. My eyes drift back to those stage stairs, the portal to the unknown.

Finally I step up and out. The lights are bright, the music is booming, and the owner narrates in a voice louder than I had anticipated. The audience is dark; I can hardly see the reported two hundred faces but I can hear them clapping and it sounds surreal. I perform my turns, remembering how I rehearsed it. Then I do a slight curtsy, walk down the steps, out into the audience and to the final backroom destination. I'm done. I can breathe again.

After the post-event hoopla, I find Jayne and we head for home.

"You did a great job," Jayne says. I have trouble believing her, but it must be true because she doesn't offer compliments very often.

***

Back at home, I drop my purse and run for the telephone.

"Yeah, it was fun, but I was so nervous. I don't know if I'd do it again. Actually, I doubt they'd ever ask me back because they want pretty people but they made an exception in my case."

"Will you knock that off? I'll meet you outside in ten minutes. I'm going to hang up and get my bike. I'll be right over."

Piper is my new best friend, a vast improvement over Crystal whom I had no trouble saying goodbye to when the father and I moved. Piper lives about ten blocks away. We like to spend our afternoons riding our bikes.

A car with a bunch of cute guys goes by. They holler and honk.

"They think you're cute, Piper," I shout.

"They were honking at *you*," she replies.

"It was you. I saw them," I counter.

"You wanna fight?" she asks.

"Yeah, I'll bash your face in," I say.

"I'm so scared," she says with friendly sarcasm.

And in the back of my mind I'm thinking, you probably should be scared, Piper. I have enough anger in me to kill you. But I don't tell her what I'm thinking because if she knew, it could be the end of our friendship. I'm not risking it.

"You don't give yourself enough credit. You think you're ugly but nobody else does. The only reason you don't have a boyfriend is because you don't have any confidence in yourself."

Piper is just being nice. She can't possibly be serious. When I look in the mirror all I see is *ugly*, me the eyesore, the oil spill on an otherwise crystalline ocean. Piper is the first person I've ever felt comfortable enough with to reveal this to. And Piper is the first person who has ever tried to tell me otherwise. I want to believe her. And maybe I do—for just a few minutes.

Piper is the best friend I've ever had. Sometimes I get irritated by her confidence, but she's sensitive and she's always trying to build me up. It's got to be annoying for her to have to constantly deal with my depression and lack of confidence. I don't want to lose her as a friend by acting stupid.

We're sophomores now. Piper and I share a locker and we've got the same lunch, so we hang out. She lives in an apartment with a pool and we had a great time this past summer when I wasn't working. Her mom is really nice and seems to like me.

"I had the weirdest dream last night." I feel like I can tell Piper these things.

"Oh, yeah?"

I nod. "Jayne was in this classroom, right? And this rowdy guy I knew from a long time ago—Hawaii, but I don't tell her that—was there and he was being his typical rowdy self and Jayne told the class, 'If you're tardy ten times, you have to *die*.' So this guy was tardy ten times and so she took him out to the garage and killed him."

"God, what a sick dream."

"I know. I have dreams like that all the time. Sometimes I think I'm going crazy."

"Yeah, right. Me, too. We're all a little bit crazy."

I laugh. Maybe it's that simple—we're *all* crazy.

We cross the street and head to For What It's Worth Records to buy our Seals and Crofts tickets. They're planning to record a live album at the Paramount so we're going to yell really loud during a quiet part of a song and see if our voices show up on the live album. How freaky would that be?

***

"I'm home," I proclaim a little too joyfully, walking downstairs to the den where the father and Jayne are watching TV.

"Where were you?" Jayne says, but I can tell she's not really all that interested. She's pissed and this feigned interrogation is merely the preamble for the ensuing rant. But I humor her with more fake joy, like I'm innocent of any wrongdoing.

"Oh, Piper and I went bike riding. We ended up at For What It's Worth to get our Seals and Crofts tickets. It started to rain, though, so we thought we'd better hurry back."

"Sit down," she says and off she goes. The father hasn't spoken a word yet. He's staring at the TV. I think he'd rather be getting a root canal.

I sit with a huff that was louder than intended, which doesn't improve things one bit.

"*We* think you're spending too much time with your friends and not enough time at home. *We* think you should be home by nine and that it would be nice if you ate dinner with us. And there are chores around here that you're neglecting."

"Okay. Can I go now?"

She ignores my request. "Your dad and I have decided that there are to be no friends in the house while we're gone, and when you go somewhere you should leave a note and tell us when you'll be back."

I think she's enjoying this.

"Okay." I'm starting to feel like a cornered feral cat. My blood pressure is rising and I can feel my face getting flushed. I'm fighting with myself to stay composed.

"And we think you should really try to be nicer to the boys. You've got an attitude that is really upsetting everyone around here."

Maybe she senses that she's pushed me as far as she should. She's not stupid. I get up, say, "Good night," And walk out. Did I say that? Yep, it came from my mouth and it was amazingly calm.

My journal pages receive the full force of my wrath. I'm the feral cat, cornered and blazing mad, screaming and screeching and clawing. How dare they? She's not even my mom and she's lording herself over me like some tyrannical ruler. She just wants to fix me because I'm *bad,* I don't measure up to her prissy standards.

All I can see are threats all around me. Jayne's malevolent attempt at trying to cage me and conform me. I hate her and her stupid rules. They just strengthen my determination to flee. *I won't be caged ever again.* I've spent my entire life dodging bullets and fists.

I can get pretty dramatic about it all—on paper. But when I talk, no one would ever know anything was wrong.

Everything is wrong and nothing is wrong.

The stepbrothers are oblivious to how close they are to serious injury. They're ignorant of the hazardous material that lies beneath my outer shell. And they're unaware of how thin and brittle that facade is and how close I am to cracking and unleashing the toxic monster-me.

I'm staring at my walls, still furious, but I remind myself that I can't explode because I've seen what my anger can do and what my rage is capable of. Images of my little brother and his bloody nose paint the bedroom walls and his terrified screams emanate from the stereo speakers.

I take my pillow and wrap it around my head to shut it out but I'm still haunted. I will never be able to reconcile the enormous guilt and anguish I feel for my little brother. I want to cut myself. It's tempting, *really tempting.* I don't think about it as much as I used to, but sometimes I can barely hold back. This is one of those times.

***

My two biggest priorities are surviving and getting a boyfriend.

The whole boyfriend dream is already several years old. Although I haven't had any formal training on the matter, there are unwritten rules where boys are concerned. Having a boyfriend is supposed to accomplish some rite of passage and is tantamount to global acceptance, like an initiation into humanity, scaling the great wall of isolation and bouncing into the land of belonging. Like until I have a boyfriend I don't really exist—and I really would like to exist.

Maybe having a boyfriend would prove that I'm worthy. Maybe it would heal the shame of past mistakes. Maybe it would nullify the "ugly" curse. Maybe it would disprove the idea that good things are for everyone but me.

Besides, all of my friends have boyfriends.

***

Piper introduces me to the world of roller skating. I hate roller skating. I'm a klutz and my sense of balance is mysteriously flawed, which is weird because I'm really good at skiing.

I'm teetering my way around the polished floor, holding on to the sideboards for dear life, while rest of the world is flawlessly floating around and around—some acrobatically—with no effort whatsoever. Great, another area in which I'm a complete and utter failure.

I leave the floor and sit on one of these round carpeted things that's supposed to pass for a chair. One of my ankles is throbbing. I'm not sure if it's because I laced up the skate too tightly or it's from that last humiliating fall I took. I heave my skate up on the carpeted seat and start unlacing. I'm admitting defeat. Besides I just saw a bunch of people from school head over to the foosball tables. I suck at foosball, too, but at least I can suck without breaking my leg.

Massaging my ankle doesn't seem to help. I can see Piper. She's one of the swans, sailing effortlessly along the floor like she was made for skating. I'm jealous. I don't want to hate Piper because she's so nice, but I have to wonder why she has it all and I have nothing.

I look toward the skate rental area and spot this super foxy guy that Piper has been pointing out. He's gorgeous and he's smiling and—holy shit—he's walking this way. He's stopping. He's looking at me. I'm going to faint.

"Don't I know you?"

"Yeah, I guess. I'm Piper's friend," I reply, trying to quell my nervousness.

"Well, wait." He reaches for his wallet, gets a pen. "Let me get your phone number."

"Are you sure you want it?" That was stupid, but I'm in shock.

Just then Piper and a couple of younger girls come over to see what's going on.

She sees his wallet, a few bills peeking out. "Wow, money!"

Super Foxy is waiting, still smiling and looking at me so I give him my number.

"I'm kind of on a natural high tonight," he says, looking deep into my melting eyes.

And at this point everyone is talking about their own personal natural high. But my high isn't so natural. Maybe I'm hallucinating and should pinch myself. Piper gives me a wink. It's time to go.

And then it's the next day and Super Foxy is calling *me*! And we're talking on the phone and it's so cool.

"Are you going skating tonight?" he asks.

"I'm not sure if I'll be able to get away. The parents are tightening the ropes and all, but I sure hope I can." I don't tell him that I loathe roller skating and he doesn't tell me that I suck at roller skating, but we both know it's true.

He tells me he hopes I'll come so we can get to know each other. And I'm thinking that this whole thing is surreal and totally far out. Finally, a cute guy interested in *me*. And for the first time in my life, I feel like maybe there is hope for me after all.

***

Piper and I are at our locker grabbing books and planning the next skating trip. I'm thinking that if I don't get stoned maybe I'll skate better and have more confidence. Pot has never been my friend but, despite the fact that I know how it affects me, I keep smoking it, hoping for a better result. "It's insane," I tell Piper.

"Your brain is eroded," Piper jokes.

"You might be right about that."

I look at my watch. "The bell's going to ring any second and I'm late. Are we meeting this afternoon?"

"Of course."

I take one final glance at Piper and wave. Now I'm walking away. This is goodbye, but I don't know it yet.

***

It's late afternoon and I'm on my bed reading, *I Know What You Did Last Summer*. Piper didn't show up today, but I tell myself it's no biggie and I remind myself of Crystal-the-control-freak and how she had to know my every move and I tell myself I will *never* treat my friends this way. Piper didn't show up. She has a good reason. She'll call or maybe I'll finish this chapter and call her. No biggie.

I can hear the phone ringing downstairs. Maybe that's Piper now. A pause and I hear footsteps coming up the stairs, a knock on the door, the door handle turning. It's the father. He stands at the door and he's got the weirdest look on his face.

"That was Carol's mom on the phone." He pauses and I'm thinking, Carol's mom? Carol lives right by Piper and she's cool, but I don't know her mom very well.

The father swallows and continues, "Piper was killed today."

I just heard the father say the most bizarre thing. Why would he joke about Piper this way? I'm suddenly in a swirling vortex of pain and panic. It's not true. The father is messing with my head. What the hell? But his countenance, that disturbed look ....

"How?" I whisper.

"She was riding her bike and she got hit by a car."

"I need to call Carol." I toss the book, stand up and float downstairs to the phone.

Carol is inconsolable. Like a drowning swimmer, she surfaces with a brief muffled narration and then plunges back into a deluge of imperceptible sadness that bounces off my hardened shell. Up and she's telling me ... the corner of 162nd and Glisan, in front of the Thriftway ... too many cars. Down, agony, sobbing. Up, "She was on her way to your house ...."

A thousand volts of emotion surge through my brain. I can't sort them out. I'm speechless. She was coming, dear God, she was coming and ... oh, shit.

I'm not crying. Carol is crying both our tears.

I'm numb.

CHAPTER FOURTEEN

Rose and I walk up the aisle. The father is following. A Churchy organ rendition of "Stairway to Heaven" drones through unseen speakers. It's a dirge that sounds beyond weird. From some far off region of my psyche, I'm assuming the planners thought this would help us remember Piper's favorite song, but it's just so weird. I can't comprehend the weirdness of it.

We find a space for the three of us. I look at the small, light green fold-over leaflet in my hand. Piper's name and birth date and the date she died are printed on the front. It's too much. It can't be real. I look ahead at the casket and flowers and her picture resting up there. It's pretty, but it's creepy.

It's all starting to hit me, the ugly, awful, undeniable truth. *Piper died.* And now, that unknown force that snuffed out my best friend's life is snuffing out mine. Sitting here, listening to the organ attempting "Stairway to Heaven" and seeing Piper's picture and seeing the little fold-over paper and all of these sad people, all of it brings me face to face with this horrific, undeniable finality. *Piper died.*

And so the blocked tears are finally flowing and flooding. I'm out of control and this place is filled with about a hundred people yet I can't stop the tears.

Piper's brother walks up behind us. He's trying to tell me something, whisper something in my ear, but I've got him in a headlock. I can't stop crying. I'm holding on because … I don't know why but I'm afraid of these tears and maybe letting go means I'll be sucked up in this tornado of emotion, heaved and bruised and tossed and dropped, bleeding and broken, into some kind of never land-point of no return.

He whispers, "My mom would like you to come into the family area and sit with us."

I'm not sure what he means. I look at the father, then I get up and I go with Piper's brother to a small area on the side of the main area.

It takes a few minutes to catch my breath and see through my tear-filled eyes. Here in the place where Piper's family is—really? Is this for real? If it is, it's the nicest thing anyone has ever done for me. I matter. I mattered to Piper and therefore I matter to Piper's family. For a second, in the midst of this unspeakable tragedy, I feel like I'm connected to humanity. *I matter.* I can't stop the tears and I can't reconcile these enormous feelings, the kindness of Piper's family mixed with this incomprehensible pain.

Some type of officiator stands at the pulpit and talks about Piper like he knows her but he doesn't and his words are overshadowed by

"Stairway to Heaven" still echoing in my head, fueling the fire in my gut. I can't seem to come to grips with any of it. I just keep crying and it's like a different me crying. A me that I can't control. It's incredibly scary. I never cry like this.

***

Life is supposed to go on and it does, but I'm lagging behind, weighted by an unavoidable, undeniable cavernous burn. Nobody tells me what grief is, how it manifests, that it's okay to be devastated and that it's a natural result of losing someone close to you. This acute ignorance fuels my feelings of inadequacy. Why can't I get it together? I just want to retreat into nothingness. Dissolve.

Right after it happened, Jayne kept telling the father, "She shouldn't be alone." But isolation was exactly what I wanted.

Jayne told me I should come with her to work. I robotically complied. It was nice that she was concerned, but I felt like an alien. Being there just added to my agony. It would have been better for me to be alone.

Piper's stuff isn't in our locker. Somebody came and got it and now our locker is empty except for my few things. *Empty.*

I'm walking, floating in a fog, from class to class. I don't really know what I'm doing here. I don't know what to say to people so they stay away and I'm alone and I want to be alone but alone is very painful here at school where Piper was so much a part of things.

Lunch is the worst. I wander tentatively by the library. Piper and I came here. There'd be a group of us seated around one of the tables and we'd banter back and forth and talk to the most receptive of the library ladies, Mrs. Connor.

She sees me standing at the door. We make eye contact and I feel her compassion so I come closer. She speaks to me about Piper and I cry. I wish she wouldn't talk because I just can't cry here in the library but I can't stop the tears.

Mrs. Connor does something for me that no one else has. Maybe it's talking, maybe it's listening, but I doubt it's listening because I'm not saying very much. I don't really know what it is she's doing but it's nice and it terrifies me. I want more of it but there is never any more.

I continue my school routine in a permanent haze. I don't fit in here—or anywhere.

Sadly, Super Foxy from roller skating slips away, another cruel twist of fate. The quest for a boyfriend has faded, however. I don't care about much of anything.

Alone in my room, I talk to Piper and I write letters to her in my journal. I tell her about this new rock group called "Boston." I want her to come back and listen to their album and tell me what she thinks.

Sometimes I'll open my desk drawer and grab the little newspaper clipping. "Biker, 15, Killed By Auto." I'll read it, thinking maybe it will somehow change things, either the event itself or my reaction to it. But nothing changes. The clipping goes back in the drawer because nothing can undo what has happened.

***

Time marches on. I've come to the conclusion that there is no reason to push on toward success and good grades and normalcy. No reason whatsoever. My best friend died at fifteen. I'm almost sixteen. I won't make it to twenty. I've known this for a long time; Piper's death just confirms it. My descent seems fitting right now. I don't possess the wherewithal for anything else.

It's the perfect fall night, no wind, no rain. The football game is in full swing but we're here to get high, looking for an obscure locale to do the deed.

Rose, me, and a bunch of other girls walk across the street and down a narrow road to an open field. It's pitch black. About fifteen of us form a circle, sit, and pass two pipes, Rose's and mine. We suck in the smoky oblivion and talk and laugh and forget everything beyond our circle, everything that exists in the darkness behind us, embracing the midnight that cradles us, this sacred place where anonymity is lavishly dispersed, where I can freely hide and where my multitude of flaws are concealed. I show my gratitude for the darkness by spending as much time here as I can.

There is this palpable unity as we sit together. It feels really good. No one wants it to end and so we stay for a long time, rapt in our own universe, talking, laughing, getting high.

Eventually we stand, stretch our legs, and start back. A splinter group trots off toward the bleachers, laughing and stumbling. Later I hear that they walked into the guys' bathroom because they were too wasted to read the sign.

"It's a free for all," Rose sings in my ear, dancing around in a pathetic, yet apropos, rendition of Ted Nugent.

Cute older guys are drinking Mad Dog by their truck, music booming. Nobody is sober tonight. I'm thinking that this is it, the perfect way to live out the remainder of my days on Earth. Everything is fun and wild and I don't have to feel anything but good.

The game is over and somebody tells us that we lost. "Who gives a fuck?" Rose blasts with irreverence. I love this about her and I can't stop laughing.

Rose and I walk back to her house since it's closer to the school than Jayne's. It's dark, save for the streetlights dispersed at regular intervals. Parents might think it pure folly to be traipsing along out here in the dark, two wasted teenage would-be crime victims, hobbling along. But we see no threats.

The darkness is a welcome entity, a life force that, when partnered with pot, propels us deeper into its world, crafted — we're sure of it — especially for us. Together, the darkness and the drug marry into a cushioned blanket, covering the stains and personal flaws and insulating us from the world's judgment and the insanity that rages out there in the world we're trying desperately to flee.

We giggle and slur a rendition of "American Pie," then marvel at the power our voices have to ignite a yellow light in a window of the house we're passing. A silhouette appears, looks and turns away, and we laugh some more and shhh each other and stumble on.

It's late. Rose's parents aren't happy but Rose is used to this "bullshit" and she just ignores them or fights back. I take notes on how to emulate her blatant disregard for authority. Where is her fear? I'm too afraid to ask her.

Rose is wild. some of our mutual friends confide in me that they're scared of her, but I believe she's harmless. I used to have this ambivalence about things, like part of me wanted to be wild like Rose but there was this other good girl part of me that worried about my future and my grades. I don't care anymore. Rose, she's a harmless wild girl and that is what I want to be, too.

The next day Rose's parents are gone and we huff aerosol Bactine and the room is spinning. We're, like, floating around laughing and our voices are outside ourselves and I'm officially initiated into the world of self-destruct and I don't give a shit.

Fortunately for her, Rose doesn't have issues with pot like I do. Despite the adverse effects, I'm rather ineffectual in my attempts to refrain from smoking it. I don't care about the ensuing paranoia until I'm stoned and going through a panic attack and telling myself I need to quit. But denial is a powerful thing.Before long, I'll repeat the cycle. Getting stoned is about more than the weed itself. It's about belonging. I like the feeling of fitting in, being accepted, being cool. If I have to get high to do it, so be it.

Rose and I are part of a nexus of teens who get stoned on the way to school, after school is over, and on the weekends, in places like the school bathroom, at friends' houses when their parents aren't home, in abandoned houses, along the trails behind the woods, behind Giorgio's, by Lloyd Center, and at the park downtown where the pimps hang out. Rose and I buy weed but I can't remember where. A bag just appears in my purse.

Between weekends, I'm back at school, going through the motions, smiling and pretending everything is cool. If only I could harness even a microscopic sliver of confidence. If only I had something solid to hold on to while the storm of doubts and self loathing rage in my head. If only there was an internal belief that I'm inherently good, decent, deserving the oxygen I consume.

My whole sophomore year is lost, except for what I write in my journal. Rose and I and usually two or three friends continue our jaunts around town because it's a trip and we both hate being home because nobody there likes us or wants us around.

I've noticed this huge chasm between the sober adults and the wasted teenagers. It's like we all avoid each other, both groups denying the other exists—or maybe just halfheartedly tolerating each other. This is how it's supposed to be, really. The adults are supposed to be sober and responsible and dedicated to normalcy, running the world and keeping us from killing each other. Teenagers are supposed to be the deviants and lawbreakers and hell raisers. We're all supposed to despise the opposing group. But occasionally, there's a breach that kind of shakes up the order of things. Like recently when one of the father's friends confided in me while driving me home. I had been babysitting for him and his wife while they were at a Black Oak Arkansas concert. He said he had a great time and, "Everyone was passing weed around."

Like some sort of cosmic crapshoot, I place my bet, but it appears more and more to be a losing game. My high won't be an escape into blissful oblivion but a trip to unfiltered hell. I've heard that acid has this unpredictable quality but nobody I know has this problem with pot except lucky me. I'm thinking that Jung or Freud or whoever could have a field day with my fucked up complexes.

I pray to God about it because there is no disputing that this whole thing is vastly bigger than I am. However, even with divine intervention, I don't think I *can* quit pot, not when all my friends are getting high and they're always offering me a hit. I've tried to quit before but success is not in my vocabulary. Besides, I'm not interested in being one of the goody kids. This group of potheads is where I fit in. Where do I belong if I quit?

KGON is playing the *Grand Illusion* album by Styx. This is really far out music. I need to buy it next payday.

It's late. I do my best thinking at night and I'm thinking that this album title is very fitting for my life. It's all been one grand illusion, I muse. "*Life* is one grand illusion," I say out loud to no one.

This reminds me of science class one day. The teacher was lecturing about the world and how it was created and how people got here. He talked about the two common theories, creation and evolution. He said that there is really no way to know for sure how it all began. Then he talked about other possible explanations.

"Maybe we were created yesterday with a memory to go with it."

There were some Christian girls seated in front of me and I could tell that the teacher's words bothered them. They're convinced that God created them and they believe the Bible's explanation. Maybe they're right. I don't know.

But my mind is massaging that other "possibility." Okay, so if I was just created with a memory to go with it, then everything I've believed about my past is a total lie because none of it really happened. In a way this would be good news, except that I've still got the memories even though they're not real memories. "Brain warp," as Piper used to say.

Wouldn't that be *the* ultimate grand illusion? To think you have a certain past but you really don't? It was all conceived and carried out by some Master Deity somewhere and you're just a pawn because you believe it and you're, like, subject to it?

And if you couldn't control your past, you probably wouldn't be able to control your future, either. It's all being controlled for you. That sucks. I mean, it doesn't give me much to look forward to because my past sucked. I'd like my future to be different.

It's kind of like I'm just floating along on some cosmic conveyor belt, being driven on my way to places that will bend and chew me, assemble me and shrink wrap me into some kind of respectable packaged adult. But it's a huge mistake that I'm here because I'm sure I won't succeed. I'm not now. How will I then?

I really should make more room for the Honor Society teens, the beautiful, popular jock and cheerleader types, the privileged, the people who will undoubtedly grow up and make the world a better place. I'm not one of them.

CHAPTER FIFTEEN

I turned seventeen a little over a month ago and, so far, there is no rescuer. No *To Sir, With Love.*

I feel like a total alien in my own home until I remind myself that it's not *my* home. It's Jayne's home and I'm the pariah.

I don't know if anyone who hasn't been in this situation can really comprehend it: feeling like a total reject or a misplaced refugee, the anathema to the rest of the household's inhabitants, the *persona non grata*—the one they all *shun.*

In a way, I kind of feel like a foster kid. My living situation changes every year or so. I can't seem to put down any roots. I can't seem to connect. I'm unable to decode the cryptic yet rudimentary bylaws of social interaction. Especially with adults—authority figures like Jayne and the father.

I don't know, maybe the whole foster kid similarity is fallacious. I mean, foster kids are sent away from their parents and, at some point, like after the parents sober up or do their jail time, there is reconciliation. I would think that there is a sense of hope in this for kids. They soothe themselves with words like, "Someday we'll be a *real* family" no matter how elusive that reality might be.

Not that I'm wishing the parents dead, but in a way it would be easier if they were. Death is final, as I've painfully learned from Piper's bike accident. If the parents were dead, I'd be forced to find my own way, just as I've had to force myself to find new friends, a new locker partner. Maybe I'd find new parents.

Death is a final goodbye, and once it happens there are no new disappointments to contend with and assimilate, only the ones that history doled out, perhaps a little too liberally.

The parents are living productive upper middle class lives, one of them right under my nose. Neither he nor the mother seems to care about any of their kids. There is no hope in this at all. No "Someday" because the parents aren't locked up in jail waiting to reunite with their kids. They're *alive* and living exactly how they want to live.

It's been almost two years now that I've been under Jayne's roof and I feel so displaced and alienated. Despite my desire to make things better, there is an inevitable wave of powerlessness and mental immobility that stymies me. I keep thinking I want to improve things with Jayne, but there is no stored up wisdom or insight that I can draw from.

I won't graduate for another year and a half, but I'm not letting that stop me. I'm not sure what I'm going to do but I'm surreptitiously looking at any and all options.

I found a phone number for a counseling center and scribbled it on a page in my journal. I might give them a call but I'm kind of scared. It's like when someone knows they need help but they're afraid of what they'll find out.

Actually, I think Jayne mistakes my quiet distance as me shunning her but it's more like my brain freezes and I just stand there in a cold, panicky sweat. I hate this feeling, but I don't know how to override it.

***

Despite my helplessness where the family is concerned, I've empowered myself by taking up running. Jayne's house is situated in the perfect neighborhood. Flat, wide sidewalks have made creating a routine almost effortless. It feels really good to move my body and stretch it to the limit. It kind of airs out my brain and I guess I really need it.

Opening the door, I'm unable to conceal my heavy breathing.

"You know, when you're out of breath, you're working too hard," greets me in a totally deadpan parlance. This is Jayne's way of saying, "Way to go. You're taking an interest in your health. Keep it up and, here, have a glass of water." But something is wrong with my hearing.

Maybe she's not taking into account that for the last five years, I've polluted my lungs with nicotine and THC and that it's going to take some time to clean them up. This is what I tell myself. Jayne doesn't know about my bad habits. Still, a little "way to go" would be nice.

I walk upstairs and into my room and there on my—Jayne's—desk is a cute Easter basket. On each side are blooming mums and in the middle is a ceramic Easter egg. Inside it is a tiny yellow ceramic chick nestled in faux straw. On my bed is a stack of clothes, washed and folded and waiting for me. I fall onto my bed, knocking over the laundry. I reach over and restack them.

Guilt. I'm such a rag. Jayne is doing these nice things for me and all I do is bitch about how much I hate living here.

I walk out and down the stairs, find Jayne.

"Thank you for the Easter basket. It's cute."

For this brief moment things are okay. Not great, but okay.

"How was your day?" she asks as she continues to fold laundry—this after she worked a full day and has dinner on the stove. More guilt.

I want to grab a pair of matching socks and fold them but something holds me back. "Okay. I'm looking for a job again. I need money."

"Well, the paper's on the table. You can check the ads."

"Okay."

While I was jogging I started thinking about getting another summer job. Sarah has been calling and it's been good to talk to a real family member. The first call was an announcement that she's pregnant. Since then she's been dropping hints about moving back to Portland after her baby is born. I'm thinking that the two of us could share an apartment if I can land a job. Then I can get out of this godforsaken hellhole.

Now all of that fresh-start shit is shrouded by my guilt.

I'll just work harder at keeping the house clean and try to come out of my room more often. Maybe that will help mend things. I could turn the music down a few decibels, too.

And I remind myself that just a few days ago I mowed the front lawn and swept the decks. I didn't think anyone noticed, but maybe the Easter basket is Jayne's way of saying thank you.

***

Rose is still wild and I'm still hanging out with her. Emily warns me to watch myself and I reassure her I am. Besides, I tell her, I make my own decisions about how much I want to fuck up my life.

I'm not so nervous about having a boyfriend anymore. I've been talking to this guy Ed for a while. He's nice but pretty damn rowdy. He lost his license for drunk driving and his job is really nothing to write home about. He's basically a classic stoner going nowhere fast, but he's nice. He's in his twenties; I like older guys.

I'm double dating at Ed's house with my friend Lauren from school and her boyfriend. The music is loud — exactly how I like it. The lights are low, inviting the darkness I crave. The table is full of tantalizing offerings.

Now it's the next day and I'm thinking about the coke and the hash and the tequila and the wild sex and thinking, shit, it all seemed fine last night while I was high.

My problem is I've got a conscience. I want to be more like Rose and just turn off everything and enjoy life. Emily keeps warning me *not* to be more like Rose. Emily is a thinker like I am — a much better thinker, at that. She's got my best interests at heart.

And so these opposing influences continue to bend and twist my brain in both directions. I think it's an identity thing. I'm not sure who I want to be or what I believe. I've thought about a final off switch but it's never more than a fleeting thought. I'm kind of hoping it will happen on its own in some random, tragic way rather than by me pulling the trigger.

The idea of seeing a shrink is still there in the back of my mind but I'm too scared to bring it to the front.

***

The break from the tensions with Jayne was indeed brief. I'm sure it's because my intentions and resolve are as fluid as the rain and subject to the mood of the moment.

Jayne is downstairs complaining to the father that I'm just sitting on my lazy ass while she's doing all the work around here. She doesn't realize that I'm working on this stupid assignment for Social Studies and that if I don't get it finished I'll flunk the class. She's always badgering me about my grades and I'm really trying to make an effort, but I can't seem to make any headway.

The father doesn't do anything, which I'm sure is pissing Jayne off even more.

Someone is coming up the stairs and … feet stomp past my door. Good. I hear Jayne's bedroom door closing. The father must not feel very well. It's rare, him going to bed at this hour.

I still feel sort of linked to the father. Other than Nellie and Sarah's intermittent phone calls and the mother's perfunctory letters, the father is really all the family I've got, and I sense there is this covert scintilla of loyalty between us that Jayne and the boys are not privy to. I'm sure it's hard for him, being in the middle, trying to make peace between Jayne and me.

Sometimes I look at him and wonder if he's not thinking this whole living arrangement is a complete disaster.

I finish my homework, finally, and run to the bathroom across the hall. I'm making too much noise and the father comes in.

"Knock off all the noise, dammit."

He must really be sick.

I make an effort to be quiet and walk back to my bedroom. I plop down on my bed and look to the door and the father is there, rage on his face.

"I told you to shut up. You're making too damn much noise!" And the gatekeeper swings open the fortress and releases the beast. Its seething energy charges toward me with fists of liberated rage. My body is demoted to an inanimate punching bag as it absorbs blow after blow. The fury annhilates my dignity and severs what little remained of our faltering family alliance.

My mind is gone, on overload. I'm paralyzed and cowering. The father's fists are striking me over and over again.

Jayne is yelling at the father to stop. She's grabbing his arms and yelling and being slung backward and losing her grip and willing herself forward again and grabbing his arms and yelling for the father to stop.

Jayne's frantic pleading eventually permeates the father's awareness. He abruptly stops and, saying nothing, leaves the room and slams his bedroom door.

I'm still on the bed, immobilized, in shock. There are no words, no wounds, just shock. I've never let the beatings hurt and I'm not going to start now.

Jayne grabs my hand. "Come on."

We're riding in the car. Neither talks.

Jayne and Rachel and even her husband Dave, who's been friends with the father since before I came back from Hawaii, are all surrounding me and I don't understand why.

Why are they asking me how I am? Why aren't they asking the father how *he* is? These are the *father's* friends, the *father's* people and they're betraying him by siding with me. They need to go to him and figure out what's wrong, not waste their time on me.

I want to get away from them.

"I'm okay," I say but it's just rote, false assurance so they'll go away, back to the father and figure out what's wrong. They really aren't helping me because they're not helping the father. All of their kind gestures are unrequited because I'm incapable of thinking.

Except that I'm feeling badly for the father.

The day's events thunder in my head. They can't be drowned out by my music because Jayne and I left in such a hurry I didn't even think to grab my radio. This disturbs me more than anything—being without my music, my distracting remedy, my comfort, my continuity, my link with a world otherwise out of reach.

Damn Jayne.

And so without really thinking about it, I allow my mind to drift past the troubling emptiness and float away on a mental rendition of Alan Parson's "Breakdown," over and over. A cool song. A prophesy.

CHAPTER SIXTEEN

Soft noises wake me out of a deep sleep. I'm out of bed before I have time to think, standing over the crib. Reaching down, I hesitate, waiting for the dizziness to pass.

Anna is so sweet and tender with her soft, ivory skin, her wispy crown, tiny fingers, and deep probing eyes. As she takes her bottle, my mind wanders to her mother. I worry about Sarah driving to work at night and how she's going to manage being a single mother. It's got to be incredibly scary. I want to make it easier for her, but I'm not sure if my concerns make it to Sarah's ears and heart.

There is abject tension between Sarah and me that wasn't there before we moved in together. We got along fine over the phone but now that we're living under the same roof there are expectations and obligations and I fear that I'm failing my sister miserably.

Without fully understanding it, we arranged for two incredibly wounded people to come together. The plan was to help each other but there is this intangible side of things that plagues me. We both have a mountain of emotional need, desperate for some kind of acceptance and family love, attempting to forge a sense of familiar belonging that has never existed for either of us. How do we produce something from nothing? How do we help each other out of the mire when we're still drowning in it ourselves?

Nothing of any substance gets voiced. That's how it's always been. We live day to day the best we know how, obliquely aware that something is missing. And when the pressure valve can no longer contain the emotions, we explode.

Anna stops sucking and starts to wiggle, so I gently remove the nipple and take the burp rag and pat her mouth. Then I rearrange her to burping position and gently pat her back. I can be a quick learner when I have to be.

Sarah is not all that different from me. She's a lonely soul looking for a place to belong in this calloused and merciless world. I'm her last resort as far as family members go and she is my last resort and, my God, what a difficult task we've imposed upon each other without even meaning to.

Determined to get the hell away from the acrimony under Jayne's roof, I moved out a few weeks ago while she, her boys, and the father were vacationing out of state. My friend Joanne owns a pickup and helped me transport my meager belongings to my new life of independence. Sometimes I wonder what Jayne thought when she climbed the stairs and saw my empty bedroom.

***

I recognize Steve right off. He lives by Rose and she told him I have the hots for him, which is just the kind of thing Rose is known for. At present, I don't have the hots for any guy.

There is a quiet confidence about him as he walks into the small restaurant and stands at the counter, waiting for me to make eye contact.

I'm befuddled and start acting giddy and stupid while filling the cup dispenser.

He smiles.

"How's it going?" I ask.

"It's good. My little brother's baseball playoffs ended tonight and his team won, so I just came from the pizza parlor."

"Oh, that's cool," I say, bending down to put the cups back on the shelf.

"Pizza and beer, always cool," he jokes. "What time do you get off? How 'bout if I pick you up?"

"I get off at nine. Sure, if you're not busy." I swallow to hold back the rising anxiety.

I'm the observer, seated above myself. Steve's arm is around a distant shoulder as the conversation below veers from one subject to another. It feels otherworldly, being here in the dark, city lights shimmering off the glassy water. It's nice, even if oddly predictable, like I saw the dress rehearsal.

There were a few guys before Steve. I thought I was in love with Dale but it ended badly and cured me of that compulsive need to have a boyfriend. I'm detached now and maybe this is why I'm observing my date with Steve from a distant point of view.

I don't have access to my history so I listen and insert replies and giggles when they're appropriate.

Steve, the perfect gentleman, opens the car door for me. His kindness is part of the script but, as the car door closes, it seals off the quixotic dream.

As we round a corner, the split-second distress siren pummels me into full-on panic. Its message is clear. "We're going off the road. We're going to die!"

A frantic impulse forces my hand toward the steering wheel to get the car back on the road, but the car hasn't left the road.

Steve must think I'm a lunatic. Shit. It happened so fast, I didn't have time to think. I just reacted to this terrifying death-vibe shrieking in my head. Although I'm still tense, I'm also embarrassed as all hell. I've never told anybody about my panic attacks and, up until now, I've been pretty good at hiding them.

Steve drops me off and kisses me good night. Because he doesn't come to my bedroom, I'm sure this is the last I'll see of him.

Sitting on my bed with my journal, I recount my day—its highs and lows. I'm pretty sure I've got my panic attack figured out. It's quite simple: I died in a car wreck at this age in a past life and I'm reliving it now in this one. It's got something to do with *quantum metaphysics*, the past and present coalescing in some kind of supernatural vortex. I read about it somewhere. It's the only explanation that makes sense. I like to think that I'm somewhat knowledgeable about spiritual things and I'm pretty sure I've got these weird panicky episodes summed up.

It doesn't dawn on me to scrutinize the pattern or that my panic might have something to do with a series of highway mishaps.

The first incident happened on the way home from the ski slopes when I was five years old. Nodding off in the backseat, I was jarred awake by a grinding, sliding motion. When the car finally came to a stop, it was resting on the opposite shoulder. The mother looked back. "Is everyone okay?" she asked, out of character. I could hear the father telling everyone that our car had hit a boulder that fell from the roadside cliff and that it was our seatbelts that saved us from careening down the hill and into the river below.

Then there was the charred evidence of the big rig explosion. And then more charred evidence of our friends dying along the road to Hilo. And Gary and his inebriated plunge into the pillar under 82nd Avenue. Then watching the red Charger-type car hitting the pole right below the father's apartment window.

I confess to my journal, yet again, that I think I need to see a shrink, but I'm still too scared.

***

School starts and I'm thrilled. Not really. I despise school with every fiber of my being. But something inside keeps pushing me, telling me I've got to finish high school.

To get to there, I've got to walk about three miles. Right now, the east wind isn't a problem, but once it starts up, dealing with it will be hell. But that's the price I have to pay for moving from Jayne's house into an out-of-district apartment with Sarah.

When school is over for the day, I rush home, drop off my stuff, and walk to work at the small restaurant on Stark Street. Earning a mere $2.35 per hour isn't affording me much spending money but I'm paying my bills and there is merit in that.

***

Steve and I are planning a camping trip. It's fall and the weather is starting to get fickle, but weather doesn't matter that much when we're planning to spend most of the time in the tent. Steve, despite my idiosyncrasies, seems to like me. He has a special campsite up by Mt. Hood that he wants to show me, so early on a Saturday we take off.

After a hearty breakfast at a highway pit stop, we drive past Government Camp and head south, through the Mt. Hood National Forest. The entire region seems weird to me, seeing bare earth devoid of its snowy carpet and huge piles of plowed remains lining the side of the road.

To keep my anxiety in check, the cassette player hums "Even in the Quietest Moments." I hike up the volume. This song, I recently concluded, is of a slightly more sophisticated caliber. It elevates itself above the silly Top 40 songs of the mid-seventies. It alludes to enlightened, encrypted messages. It propels the listener inward to make the discovery. I find it irresistible.

I'm trying to convince Steve to listen closely to the lyrics but he resists.

"You won't find the meaning of life by listening to a bunch of pothead musicians," he says with a smile.

"Listen," I argue, "who do you think 'Dear' is, some banal love interest or something more cosmic like God? The whole song seems celestial in nature, too theatrical to be a simple come-hither love story, don't you think?"

"We can't know who 'Dear' is because it's intended to be a mystery, like most poetry. And besides, the musicians are stoned."

Fitting, really. Like life. Too much mystery. Stoned or sober, life is a trek through a pitch-black room, stumbling over injustices, maneuvering blindly around bullies and blunders, dusting off the pain, licking the wounds, picking the scabs, remembering where the trouble spots are in hopes of a danger-free future. It's all so deep and philosophical. Steve and I discuss it like we really know something and I like this about Steve. Despite his reluctance for interpreting song lyrics, he knows things.

At a certain point there is a sign that reads "Timothy Lake," so we turn and head down a slightly narrower road.

Towering Douglas firs whiz past, jutting skyward, shading the golden autumn sunlight. Scattered scarlet-leaved vine maples punctuate the forest floor. Seeing them makes me melancholy since they're a stark reminder that the sun's warmth is on the wane. Now that I'm no longer a skier, I have no reason whatsoever to like winter. I dread the cold. I loathe winter.

We see the lake and stop for a look around. The air has a distinctly clean, piney smell. I take a few deep breaths and stretch my cramped legs.

The lake, mirroring the blue sky above, is a huge catchment pool for the runoff that meanders alongside the pointy firs that grace the hundreds of foothills, squeezed between the preeminent structures like Mt. Hood itself, Mt. Jefferson to the south, Mt. St. Helens to the north.

Steve takes my hand and we walk down to the lakeside.

"In the summer this place is packed with people," he tells me.

I try to imagine kids running around, the scent of smoky campfires, the sound of music blaring, but it's quiet today. The silence is duplicitous, putting me slightly on edge as the unseen hand switches the "What if...?" tape to the "on" position.

Ignoring it, I kiss Steve and he responds by joking about getting inside my pants right here and now. I laugh and fake-slap him.

Driving on, we cross a narrow bridge and turn onto a gravel road.

Tawny grass borders the roadsides, lying sideways as if anticipating the heavy snow that will weigh it down in a few short weeks. Pockets of sunshine and shade alternate, and every now and then we can spot a stream down below or off in the distance to our left. The farther we go, the more the valley envelops us and the closer the stream gets. And the heavier my anxiety feels.

After about two miles of windy road, Steve turns the car around, pulls over as close to the shoulder as possible and parks.

When camp is set up, we eat a meager dinner, then, with the coming darkness, settle inside the tent for the night. I can hear the hypnotic *tick-tick* of rain drops splattering against the thin canvas. They won't leave me alone. I keep telling myself it's just rain, steady, constant *rain*.

"It's just rain? Okay. But maybe not." The Shadow, having emerged as a fully palpable apparition, is causing me to question my reality.

"No, it's just rain."

"Fire."

"Rain. It started before we even got in here."

"Fire. And it's getting closer. Can't you hear it getting louder? See the flames?"

"Rain."

"Fire. You'd better check."

"I'm okay."

"You're going to die—burn to death."

I'm broken, my mental reasoning swallowed up in a zipper-grabbing frenzy. I'm positive there is a crackling fire surrounding the tent, inching its way closer to my helpless form trapped inside this tiny tent. I've got to get out of here!

I fumble onto the dirt, scattering fir needles every which way. My knees and then my shoeless feet freeze against the wet ground. I'm dizzy, shaking, rubbing my icy hands. Steve scuffles out behind me, rises and points to the fire he built a few hours earlier. It's dying, a victim of the steady rain now dripping down the back of my neck and off my nose.

The undisputed rain—how could I have mistaken it for fire? It splatters off the tent canvas beside us and tree branches that tower over us as the landscape drinks up the deluge.

What was I thinking?

Steve's arms are around me and his words are a balm that forces this bizarre netherworld to recoil like a threatened snake back into the shadows of my psyche.

In the tent, the rain persists, while I labor to fuse Steve's rational point of view with mine. If I'm going to get over my anxiety, I'm going to have to absorb everything I can from Steve, think like he thinks, armor myself with pragmatic realism. Replace my inordinate teenage paranoia with a stockpile of adult salvo, a store of artillery at the ready to shatter an unseen enemy. And to clinch my internal agreement, I'll have to get serious about quitting pot. It's really screwing with my head.

***

Okay, so no consuming fire, but there might be a bear or a psychopath on the loose. While Steve and I are alone in the woods, this enemy feeds off our perceived vulnerability.

"What if … what if…?" foists itself into my consciousness in a steady stream, as steady as the one I cast my line in to but don't catch anything, because I'm lousy at fishing, preoccupied.

What if a bear attacks me? Or worse, what if it attacks Steve, ripping his body to shreds with its razor sharp teeth?

What if a man comes through here? He seems nice at first and we make friends with him, but he's really a psychopath, and he ties us up and tortures us or kills us with his rifle. Or worse, a butcher knife.

I tell myself I've got to listen to these scenarios because they *could actually happen* and *when*—not *if*—they do, I need to be prepared. I need to have a firm getaway plan.

So, my mind is divided between what's outside me, nothing but a really pleasant camping trip, and what's inside me: "danger, danger!"

I'm getting weary. I didn't expect this. It takes an enormous amount of effort to pretend everything is great when it's not.

I seem to have lost all last night's resolve to think like Steve.

***

It didn't take long to realize that Steve is totally different than the superficial guys of my past. He's genuine and we have intelligent conversations. Maybe I'm doing his ego a favor since he knows more about the world than I do. But my gray matter is very sponge-like and, because I'm so devoid of perspectives, I genuinely welcome his.

"I'm just a natural born worrier, a naturally paranoid person," I confess as we walk.

"I think it might be because you've had a lot of things go wrong in your life," Steve says, squeezing my hand.

"I have things a lot better than some people," I counter.

Actually, I haven't given much thought to just how *wrong* things have gone. I'm telling myself that my disappointments are trivial. Besides I don't want to feel sorry for myself. The mother was always talking about how wrong it is to feels sorry for yourself. Later, as I write in my journal, it dawns on me that Steve told me *why* I'm a worrier, but he didn't tell me how to overcome it. But maybe it's because I didn't ask him. Instead I trivialized the whole thing, taking my cues from a distant mother. And maybe it's because I'm too scared of what Steve might say.

"Bad thoughts are satanic," I write in my journal.

At the urging of Steve's friend Monte, we've been going to church. Although I don't really fit in, the people are nice and the things the pastor says are helping me get an idea of what Christianity is all about. It's warfare—good versus evil.

The pastor says, "When the bad thoughts come, just pray, 'Lord, please don't let me think these awful things. I believe in you. I have faith in you.' Then God will come through."

If only it were that easy. It doesn't matter how much I pray. Inside, my brain is always reciting the "What if" speech—or worse. Sometimes I envision horrific, gruesome, unmentionable things.

There are books on the subject that I think I need to read. When I was younger, I longed for a rescuer, someone to take me far, far away and love me and cure my despondency. Now that Steve and I are going to church, I can see that God is sort of like a rescuer. He doesn't really take us away from everything bad but supposedly he helps us think about things differently. At least this is what the pastor says. Maybe if I hang around long enough I'll figure it out.

***

It's awkward here at Jayne's house. When she and the father invited Sarah, baby Anna, and I to Christmas brunch, I cringed. But Sarah really wanted to give the father a chance to see his granddaughter, so I reluctantly agreed.

The same pictures hang on the walls, same furniture, same smells. Although it was only last summer that I gathered my things and left for good, it feels like a lot longer. My life is so different now. But at Jayne's, where nothing has changed, I feel like I'm being sucked back into a somber cave.

The stepbrothers make a perfunctory appearance, obviously at Jayne's insistence. But quickly enough, they're off to other places, validating the persisting tension.

Jayne is in the kitchen preparing the food. Although it's a strain, I'm choosing to focus on the good in Jayne. She *is* good. It was just the circumstances that were bad.

As I sit on the sofa, Jayne's abstract painting stares back at me from the adjacent wall above the stereo. It's always been there, hanging in that place, complementing Jayne's chic and trendy color scheme. It doesn't let on exactly what it is, which makes people stare and wonder and contemplate, cocking their heads to one side as if maybe a different perspective will reveal its mystery. It's just blobs and splashes and swishes of pretty paint colors, but surely it depicts something obscure, shadowy, and only vaguely recognizable. A box, maybe.

A lot like my life. A bunch of blobs and splashes and swishes and boxes, all only vaguely recognizable and remarkably easy to trip over.

The clanking of dishes serves to quicken my manners. I should help Jayne but I'm plastered to the sofa, trying to make small talk with the father. Just the suggestion of skiing will usually do the trick. He'll take off like a rocket with musings about the abysmal snowfall or the latest Warren Miller film or how many times he's been up to Mt. Hood this winter.

While engaging the father, I can't help wondering how different things might have been had I come to live with Jayne at, say, nine or ten, when I was still young, impressionable, and needing a mommy to protect me from the thunder, when I could have latched on without any preconceived prejudices or defense tactics.

Fifteen was a bad time to throw us together. By then I was already full of pain and anger and rebellion. Primitive and uncultured, undomesticated, my claws were at the ready to scratch and tear anyone who dared venture too close.

Teenage angst clouded mature thinking. All I could see was the negative: Jayne's agenda—or what I assumed was her agenda— the *improvements* I sensed she wanted to impose; her desire to mold me into a good person because I was so very bad.

There's no doubt I was—and am—bad. But Jayne was supposed to tell me I was good. But she didn't, or, if she did, I was too bad to listen.

I'm pretty sure Jayne would have clicked with that nine year old me, because at nine, I was good and Jayne wouldn't have felt the need to improve me or, if she did, I would have been too naïve—too good—to know it.

I want to thank Jayne for trying. I want something, some tool to cut through the ice between us but I'm frozen in confusion and helpless fog. Nothing of any value is verbalized or legitimized. I'm as guilty the father and Jayne because, just like them, I'm not offering anything of substance. It seems tension is as much a permanent fixture as Jayne's abstract painting.

***

Once the worst part of Christmas is over, the best part begins. Steve ushers me through the front door. His mother and three brothers greet me with friendly smiles. I grin back sheepishly as Steve steers me over to the sofa in front of a large box, his Christmas present for *me*.

I'm nervously trying to say and do the right things so these people I'd like to impress will label me "Normal." But the harder I try, the more inebriated I feel.

"Open it," Steve tells me, all giddy. He reverts to a six-year-old-at-Christmas and he's really cute. His smile briefly restores my calm and, as I look from him to this huge gift, I smile back. He's obviously put a lot of effort into it. It's so nice, too nice. It's scary. I've never told him that I can't do this, so he thinks I can, but I can't.

Steve's brothers and mother are watching, also excited to see me open the box. But other than a brief once-over, I can't look at them.

I unwrap the box, and inside is another wrapped box, only slightly smaller. Then inside it, is another and then another, all slightly smaller than the previous. And finally, in the tiniest box, nestled within a velvet box is a ring. Steve's gift to me.

Everyone is watching me. I'm sure they're judging me but I'm trying to ignore them so I can function. Then I remind myself that it's rude to ignore people and the confusion shoots another syringe of numbness into my bloodstream.

I take this sweet gift and give it to Steve and he puts it on my finger. I give him a peck on the lips and a hug while everyone is still watching. I'm wishing I could feel something genuine but nervousness has robbed me of my joy.

Steve's mom has been cooking all day and the savory aroma that orbited when I arrived has entered my atmosphere. There is a place setting for me, which confirms something cryptic.. I feel a mixture of gratitude and fear.

I can relax a little now that all eyes are off of me. Steve's mom, like Sarah, is a skilled cook and it's all I can do to keep from devouring what's before me.

There is family chatter and laughter. Stress and animosity are strangely missing. Weird. Pleasant.

What if they ask me to talk? What would I say? I don't exist outside of right now because everything that is remotely *me* has slipped into some kind of obscure cerebral pocket, out of reach. All that remains is this flesh and bones shell. There is no me. So I sit and smile and offer a pretend comment now and then because that is what you do if you want to be accepted by people. Mostly smile and listen.

CHAPTER SEVENTEEN

Sarah and I stand at the sliding glass door, looking into the distance. The leaden February morning sky offers no hint of what's to come, but, behind us, the TV announces that reporters are "standing by" at some location in Washington State where the skies are clear. They're saying it should happen at about ten minutes after eight, which prompts Sarah and me, in unison, to look at the clock. Time seems to stand still while we're waiting ... and ... waiting ...

"I think it's happening."

"I think so." Sarah is never very excitable. Even with me, her spastic sister, beside her, she remains calm. I admire her even temperedness. I tell myself I need to be more like her, starting now, but I've said this so many times. For some peculiar reason, it doesn't seem to stick.

"It's definitely getting dark. Look, the streetlights are coming on."

After a few seconds, there is no question about it. A short period of twilight seques to midnight darkness.

Sarah and I stare, moderately awed.

We hear the TV and glance over. Cameras with highly filtered lenses are pointing toward the sun and the undeniable silhouette of the moon migrating smack dab in front of it. The reporters tell us this is the only way we can safely observe this *total solar eclipse.*

But it's more fun to look outside. It looks just like any typical night, but only for a little while, and then we detect daylight again, and in just a few more minutes, the confused streetlights click off and daylight once again declares supremacy.

"That was pretty cool," we both agree.

And that is about as pleasant as it gets between Sarah and me.

***

There was an undocumented agreement that when Sarah uprooted herself and moved to Portland she and I would do lots of things together. I would introduce her to my entourage of acquaintances and she'd be included in my comings and goings and would form friendships of her own and feel like a part of things.

Then Steve entered my life.

Now I'm torn. I've got Steve and things are great between us. He occupies my thoughts and my emotions and any free time we both might have. We've fallen head over heels in love. I'm constantly asking myself what I did to deserve such a great guy.

But there is very little time or energy left for Sarah and I feel this tremendous guilt over placing her at the bottom of my list, below Steve, school, job and friends.

I feel guilty when I go off with Steve somewhere and she's left by herself to take care of Anna.

I feel guilty over placing my own needs above hers. And for being happy when I know she's not. I admit I've never really been the rescuer type. I really wanted to help my sister, but I don't think I possess the tools for such an altruistic endeavor. I'm too selfish.

Sarah has always been the better sister, selfless, giving, calm, and rational. I'm an ingrate, detached and self serving. It seems that our antithetical temperaments emphasize my own failures. And now that I've been rescued by Steve, I want to rescue Sarah—but I don't know how.

***

The east wind is on a rampage and making it very difficult to walk to school. I suppose it's all science, cold fronts or whatever, but I'm taking it very personal as it assaults my face. Maybe this is a cosmic punishment for being so mean to Sarah and for being such a selfish, pigheaded egomaniac.

There is a lull in the oncoming traffic so I look behind me and for a second my skin tingles its thanks for the reprieve. No cars coming, so I dart across the five lane strip, hop up to the sidewalk, and increase my stride, mindful of the bell's ring and the threat of that dreaded tardy slip.

I always hope that by walking on this side the trees will serve as a windbreak, but, once again, the east wind proves itself impervious to such things. I keep walking, looking down at my feet. My ears are frozen from frigid air continually roaring past them. It stings my eyes and makes my nose run. I'm sure my mascara is gone, or more likely masked beneath my eyes, making me look like a raccoon—or Alice Cooper. Hopefully, once I get to school, there will be enough time to make a brief side trip to the bathroom.

The mother's last letter said that Adam is staying with the scary aunt and the scary uncle. Shit. This can't be good, but maybe things are different for him than they were for me. Maybe the scary uncle has mellowed out or something.

Sarah and I have been discussing the idea of having Adam live with us. Money is the biggest issue. Well, that and we'd have to get a bigger place but that's not really a problem because the apartment complex next door has three bedroom units so we wouldn't have to move very far.

Rounding the corner, my icy toes dodge a puddle; a building briefly shelters me from the worst of the wind. Ironically, I feel hot. I take my hand out of my pocket and wipe my runny nose and make a mental note to have about six Kleenexes in my pocket for future walks.

Eventually the wind will get bored and rain will set in, which will be an improvement but will leave me with a different set of vain predicaments in front of the bathroom mirror before getting to class.

***

The mother has come to see me graduate. She smiles and smokes. Her blue ribbon companion is still impervious to gravity and rises as it always has to hug the ceiling in a toxic cloud, reminding me that some things are compulsory and bound by the rules of nature and will never change.

Everyone is ill at ease because the invisible elephant in the room keeps us from getting too close to anything remotely resembling a real family. Our dialog is always superficial.

There is a senior all-night party but this compulsion to escape my classmates and the old life that they represent can't be ignored. I'd rather be with Steve.

So, without the slightest hesitation, I slam and latch the door to my old life once and for all and forge ahead to better things.

***

The apartment door closes with a thud. I fiddle with the knob to make sure it's locked, hoping I didn't wake Sarah and Anna.

As I walk to the bus stop, the sight of the ashen sky doesn't help my mood. It's June. I was hoping for sunshine to mark the day I start my new job and my new life.

An older woman walks up and stands with me. Neither of us speak. We look to the east and wait for a bus that should be here by now.

She sits a few seats in front of me, obviously well-versed in this morning procedure. I'm the floundering newbie taking notes. Sporting jet-black hair with a few artfully staged lines of gray, she's provocative in her designer clothes and matching shoes and handbag. She probably subscribes to *Vogue*. Unbeknownst to her, she keeps my mind buffered from the contrived dangers of a bus ride to work.

The bus crosses the bridge and I hold my breath. Then it sways and glides into downtown.

At Yamhill Street, I grab my purse, make my way off, and notice that the *en vogue* woman has already disembarked and is walking up the same street, entering the same building, stepping into the same elevator. I get off on the seventh floor. She keeps going.

I'm told what my duties are: keep tabs on the comings and goings of lobby activity and take phone messages. To pass the time, one of the girls gives me a bunch of telephone slips to match up to clients for billing purposes.

It's ten o'clock when someone comes to relieve me while I go up one flight to relieve the main receptionist. To my surprise, seated at an exact replica of the seventh floor desk, is the *en vogue* woman from the bus stop.

Later, at home, I can't help think how weird it is that of the literally hundreds, maybe thousands of bus stops and the hundreds maybe thousands of businesses in the Portland metro area I just happen to be at the same stop headed to the same place as the other receptionist at this new job.

And so my new life catapults me into the adult world of high society. At nineteen, I'm a fish out of water, adapting and hiding—or at least trying to hide—my plethora of inadequacies.

Without overseeing the construction, I've managed to build a fairly impenetrable wall separating my work world from the rest of my life. There is inherent shame over feeling so phony and dirty and inadequate, as well as a fear of being found out for the hollow wannabe I am. What was I thinking, entering this sane world where I'm so clearly *not*?

My list of *don'ts* is growing exponentially. My co-workers are always bantering and making evening or weekend plans. It's awkward for me to constantly decline their friendly invitations, but the fear of exposure is terrifying.

***

When Adam comes to live with Sarah and me, my high hopes for helping him and forging the makings of a real family are quickly dashed by heartbreaking reality.

Adam is painfully quiet. Something isn't right. I want to talk to him but there is a wall between us that seems impenetrable. He stays in his room way too much and Sarah and I suspect that he's skipping school.

If that isn't enough, the financial pressures are difficult. It blows me away that neither parent feels it their duty to contribute a cent toward our endeavor, our wellbeing, our *survival*. It wasn't easy to swallow my pride and grovel but I did, under the erroneous pretense that the parents actually gave a shit.

I have my theories. The mother figures she's had to support Adam for years and it's high time the father pitch in, step up and be a dad. The father, staunchly adhering to the legality of it all, decides that with the custody agreement, it's the mother's *legal* duty to foot the bill, abdicating himself from any obligations whatsoever. Neither of them will actually utter *words* to the other, and they both seem to be mysteriously short of cash these days.

Maybe this is payback for emancipating ourselves. Maybe they're both thinking, "You wanted to be independent, now live with it," which is fine. Sarah and I have been living with it and doing quite well, all things considered. But now that we have Adam—*their* dependant minor—we could use some help from the people that birthed him, especially since they seem to have plenty of money for cruises, ski trips, new cars, and every other luxury under the fucking sun. It's the principle of it.

But parental selfishness renders Sarah, Adam, and me abandonded once again, like Prissy's kittens left alone in a field so long ago. We're ignored, maybe even shunned, by the woman and the man who at one time, in a weak moment of stupidity or passion or a combination of both, pledged their love to each other. And yet it's been nothing but mutual disdain for as long as I can remember.

Adam knows that we're financially strapped and I fear he believes he's an intrusion.

Eventually the nomadic, traumatized, victimized young man, who just needs stability and parents to love and care for him, leaves us and continues to get tossed around like a bag of garbage.

For years I've held a marginal apathy for the parents, conceding that this is just how things are with them. They're not interested in being parents; they're distant, aloof and masterful at making their own needs and desires highest priority. But now, apathy has been usurped by full-blown *despising*. It's bad enough that they pulled their shit on Sarah and me, but seeing it all centered on Adam really brings it home. I still remember that little blond-headed boy romping on the green grass, giggling happily between puppy tongue licks. It was a Pepsi commercial, but it was real, too. And it intensifies that familiar emotional agony that I fear is becoming a lifelong fixture.

How can the mother and father not see that they have a duty to their offspring? How can they be so uncaring? Why are we such unworthy kids?

***

The main difference between the municipal buses and the school buses is the driver's impatience. He's got a schedule to keep. As I tromp back to an empty seat, the bus driver accelerates and for just a second the bus's forward motion and my backward motion coalesce and I hover in one spot. There is probably a scientific name for this principle. Maybe I'll ask Steve if I remember. He's so smart and understands stuff like this.

The *en vogue* receptionist, Margaret, and I are friendly now, sometimes sitting together, sometimes not. She's been a career woman for many years and flawlessly makes the rounds with her stockpile of social graces. She's well-liked and respected at work, difficult shoes for lowly me to fill.

If my anxiety is manageable, I might read a book to fill the solitary commute, but those times are becoming fewer and fewer. Drivers will take the corners faster than I think they should or accelerate faster than I believe is safe. I go nuts inside with missives of danger and doom. I'm going to die, crushed under the weight of the bus. I'm hoping that none of the other riders picks up on my fear. Sometimes I'll glance around and wonder why everyone else seems so at ease.

In the meantime, Steve wraps up his college studies, begins his career, and we start planning our wedding. I've been enmeshed in my double life for so long, I hardly think twice about it.

***

The wedding is going superbly except that I've got all these people from my fractured world gathered together. It's just too weird to wrap my mind around. The *family people*—Steve's and mine, which is strange enough—but then there's the *church people* and the *work people* and the *high school people*—all here swimming around in this bubbly social pool. The walls I've laboriously created to delineate these groups have vaporized. I've got an underlying fear that each group is unhappy with the other groups and they might start a major brawl or something. It's a helpless feeling. Even though I'm the bride, I can't fix it. I'm responsible to keep everyone happy, employ tactical crowd control, entertain everyone. *I'm the bride*. I'm on mental overload and I keep going back and forth, mentally debating myself.

Weddings are stupid, at least when the bride is me.

Maybe everyone is happy, I don't know. I don't care. *I'm* happy, so they can all go to hell.

Steve and I are ready to leave the church. I've changed out of my dress, Steve out of his tux. Most of the people are outside waiting for us to descend the church steps and parade to Steve's decorated Mustang so they can toss the traditional bird seed.

That is what you're supposed to do.

The whole wedding is like this—doing what I'm *supposed* to do. So I just smile and play the role.

"Here goes." Steve grabs my hand and we walk out and stop. My eyes quickly scan the crowd. A few of my bridesmaids are here on the steps. They're all talking at once, looking at me, looking at Steve. I can't hear any of them.

Rose is wielding a cigarette so I hold up my hand and she hands it to me. I breathe in the nicotine and it hits my bloodstream and my head. Cigarettes always make me nauseous and dizzy. Why do I smoke?

Because when I'm around Rose, I smoke. Always.

The crowd has thinned. People have left but I can't tell who remains because I can't seem to zero in on them. They're sort of scattered around the parking lot, standing in the shady places because it's getting hot this afternoon.

I focus on Steve's car. I've got to get away from all of this.

I should have opted for a small wedding, a few friends.

No, it was great just the way it was. How can I think such a thing? Regrets? No way.

Steve drives us to the hotel. I'm a different person now, a *married* person. I like this new role. I like that I'm not alone anymore.

My arm is stretched and resting on the back of Steve's seat. I'm stroking his hair. It's okay for me to touch another human being.

Between our brief silences, I'm thinking how stupid it was that I took a drag off Rose's cigarette. The church people don't know I smoke.

***

I love my new routine. I get up early and start the coffee and fix Steve's meals. We go to work and come home and make love two or three times a night. I tell myself that as long as Steve gets plenty of *me*, our relationship will be just fine. Men like a lot of sex.

Steve and I will not dissolve. We're not like other couples who divorce for a variety of reasons. Our marriage will always be strong. Sometimes Sarah implies that she doesn't think we'll last. She thinks I can do better. I don't know what she's talking about.

She comes to visit and brings Anna, who toddles around with her books or her blankie, looking adorable in a dress Sarah made for her.

After they leave, I think about how difficult Sarah's life is contrasted with my easy street. It seems so unfair, she and Adam and their monumental struggles. I feel a horrific sense of guilt because I have it so good. It wasn't very nice of me to forsake them for my own happiness, just like the mother did.

CHAPTER EIGHTEEN

"Did you feel that?" The words are out of my mouth before I know what hit me.

Things are amiss. The nightmares that I've spent the better part of ten years coping with show no signs of letting up and the panic attacks are increasing dramatically. Here at work there are times when it feels as if the whole building is shaking or swaying and this causes my adrenaline to shoot through the roof. I blurt my panic and immediately regret it. I'm a very private person and hate the thought of exposing my vulnerabilities.

Janette brings me information on hypoglycemia. Since refined sugar exacerbates the symptoms, I eliminate it from my diet. Anything to stop the agony. And to stop the building from swaying.

I start jogging again. The neighborhood to the west of the apartment complex is perfect with quiet streets and level sidewalks. Before long I've got the whole place memorized.

Steve and I continue to go to church. The people are friendly but I'm cautious and guarded, trying to fit in without revealing too many personal details. It's easy, actually, since I can't access my personal essence when I'm in the company of others.

***

Moments turn into months and then years. Our backyard is typical suburban fare. Enclosed with a six foot tall wood fence, it more than adequately partitions us from the neighboring yards. While my daughter naps, my son innocently takes domain of his corner, carving roads and digging holes with a shovel just his size. I reassure myself that he can't get out. He's not going to wander down the street and get hit by a car. He's safe.

I'm no longer a fraud in the broadest sense. I'm a mother with a toddler and a baby. This role fits like a glove, like a Band-aid taped over the festering sores of my past. My kids are my life, my reason for living. I love them with every fiber of my being. I love them so much it hurts. I can't let them out of my sight because I don't trust people. I'm terrified that someone is going to take my babies from me.

It's not enough that the fence is tall. I must watch my precious boy because a psycho pedophile or someone who wants to see me suffer could jump the fence grab him and be miles away before I even know he's missing. The thought sickens me. In my mind, possibilities are *probabilities*—if it *can* happen, it *will* happen. I must always stay on guard.

Steve wonders what's happened to his wife. I hate sex and I worry all the time. He doesn't know that the nightmares are at full throttle and that I'm starting to get really angry and that I keep seeing myself torturing our kids.

I try to put a smile on my face and remind myself that I've got a great life—two wonderful kids, a nice house, a great husband, financial independence—a great life. So how can I utter even the smallest complaint about anything? I have no right. All I have to do is look at Sarah or Adam to see how good I've got it. Somehow I ended up with the prize, the undeserved mega jackpot. So I need to quit feeling sorry for myself. And I've got to try to make time for Steve. He's feeling really hurt that I'm not more emotionally connected to him like I used to be.

***

I've been here a thousand times, caught in this somnolent world between worlds, suspended in an indefinable vortex. Not asleep but not awake, it starts as a warning of sorts, a faint harbinger of what's to come. Even if I could, there's no time to react. Immediately I'm consumed, paralyzed by an electrical force that envelops me in a cocoon of terror. Trying to escape seems to exacerbate the agony. I can't move. I can't wake up.

A mind game of "yes-no" plays in my brain while volts surge through my body, simultaneously pleasuring me and terrifying me. Interminable, it wears me down and I say yes, because in this world ambivalence is not tolerated. And I'm completely seized by a malevolent orgasmic consummation.

One evil becomes legion. Like a hive of angry bees, they encircle me, buzzing around my head in some kind of frenzied dervish, whispering words I can't understand, a fracas of thousands swarming, murmuring, chanting. And they beat against my eardrums and squeeze me so tightly that I feel like I'm in a box and I can't move or breathe. They try to shove me off the bed, onto the floor.

"Jesus," I scream, remembering the words of the pastor.

I've *become* what is encircling me. I am malevolent hatred. It's me and I'm It. We're fused. It's not human. Or if It is, it's the foulest, vilest most vicious form of humanity one can fathom and I'm It.

I tell myself to wake up. "Wake up. Wake yourself up." I know Steve is over there and yet he's a million miles away. I can't get to him so he can wake me up.

I never know how or when it leaves or even *if* it leaves. But I wake up in the morning in the same bed. I can barely remember most of it, which makes it easier to put it out of my mind.

Steve asks, "What's wrong?"

"I had another nightmare." But I downplay it because it's part of that other life, that covert Kafkaesque part of me. They happen fairly regularly, in varying degrees of intensity and duration. I've had them since I was fourteen.

***

I am pregnant again. It's been five years and I'm ready for another baby. I'm almost thirty. Steve is excited, too.

I feel a strong curiosity about my origins. I wonder what life must have been like when I was a baby. What the mother went through, what kind of baby I was. There are so many questions I want to ask her as I try to visualize my tiny form growing inside the mother's womb—a stranger's womb—the body of a woman I don't know, but maybe this doesn't have to be the case.

My baby is breech, just as I was. But the doctors are more skilled and more careful about infant trauma now. Everything goes smoothly and, despite my emotional bruises, there are no bruises on my infant daughter.

The mother makes another brief, perfunctory appearance. When she got here, I sheepishly prohibited her blue ribbon companion, but now I feel guilty. It won't be long before she has to go outside and light up and the weather isn't very compatible for such endeavors. She's got the scary aunt with her, though, so they can smoke together.

I have so many questions. I feel this compulsion to bond with this woman who birthed me, this beautiful woman who is a complete stranger, who signs her letters, "Love, Mom," but never *says* I love you and never writes anything of substance in those letters, just includes an obligatory check around Christmas and birthdays. Is she saying it and I'm just not hearing it?

I'm that kid again.

"Tell me how I was born," I demand from the backseat as the mother shuffles Sarah, Adam, and me off to somewhere.

She takes a long drag, returns the cigarette to the pullout ashtray. The blue ribbon rises. I'm too far back for my breath to blow it sideways so I just watch it squiggle as it goes up and wait for the mother to speak.

She's brisk. It's a paraphrase, "Stormy night, breech, black and blue, seven pounds, seven ounces." Perhaps more is said but lost beyond my nascent attention span.

Her words are music and sing of my genesis. My inception. Nobody else's. My skin and what lies beneath it is wrapped up in the mother's paraphrase.

There are similar glimpses when the mother feels so inclined. The occasions are rare and the speeches are guarded so if I want to know—and I do—I've got to seize the moment, be quiet and listen.

She hints at "missing out."

She alludes to her mother's moroseness. "If I upset her, she wouldn't talk to me for days."

And, just like that, there is a brief alliance, a mother/daughter bonding. Sarah and me and now the mother, all agreeing that the grandma is mean and grumpy.

They're very similar women, the mother and the grandma. How many generations back does the familial pattern go, I wonder.

Seated on the sofa, the mother and the scary aunt complete each other. They're sisters-in-law but more like blood-sisters, the closest of friends, Oprah and Gayle. I've always been jealous of their relationship.

The mother is quiet, mildly fidgety. Her countenance is polite but only offers a surface rendition of friendliness that illuminates rather than bridges the gap between us. The elephant. It hurts me deep inside, but I hide it and mirror my own rendition.

The familial pattern?

She hands me a time-worn and water-damaged baby book. Tattered binding and faded pink pages reveal my history in tidbit form. A newspaper clipping with the doctor's identity and the vital statistics; a few sixties-era baby congrats signed by people I don't know; a few blurry black and whites.

I'm not sure if the mother thinks I'd like it or she doesn't want it. Maybe both.

The aunt effortlessly fills in the mother's silences. At my bidding she reminisces briefly about old times. Two close calls.

"There was that time you and Norbert wandered out onto the highway. And then there was the time you and Sarah were roughhousing in your grandpa's car and somehow that car started rolling and went all the way to the bottom of the hill with you trapped in it."

The aunt speaks with a distinct edge in her voice that reveals something akin to annoyance. "You were such a bother. The whole thing was your fault because you were such a brat." She's not saying these things, but they're what I hear; a history of petulant tones airdropped into my unguarded gullibility, commandeering my guilt and self loathing and failure. I smile. I'm numb. The wall is thick. The familial pattern.

The mother and aunt seem oblivious. They've long since abdicated themselves from it all. What's done is done. It was thirty years ago. They sit across from me smiling, talking of their plans to visit Australia.

The mother hands me my daughter. I willingly take her. She's my baby and I love her with a consuming devotion that can't be measured and can't be separated from my essence. It's who I am, this baby's mother, a role I joyfully and completely embrace.

Standing here, holding the next generation, I'm straddled—or more like huddled—between the years.

I attempt a brief look into the mother's eyes. There is no denying that the thread is broken. It was severed years ago. She dismissed me at thirteen, releasing both of us from what little there was to begin with.

And now that I'm face to face with my loss, a sense of desperation wells up, a need to glue the strings, tie the loose cords that have undergone a decade of aimless bashing and jolting by the elements of time and egos and pride and misunderstandings.

Like wanting to dam up the flow of water, I want to stop the inevitable, keep something more valuable than gold from walking out door. I'm paralyzed by my own devastation. The culmination of wounds, like the smoldering volcano of years ago, threatens to erupt and spill its insides over the land.

I can't contain it. "Don't leave," I cry.

"Don't leave Mom. I'm scared."

Tropical thunder rattles the meager shell of a house. I'm only nine and in panic overdrive. But she knows how dramatic I can be. She's got plans.

My walls have crumbled and I see what's been missing. I want it. I want a mother. I want to connect. I want to find my roots. Maybe I just want to know that I was a wanted baby and that I was loved, that I mattered. I don't remember any of that and I'd like to know if it's just a memory lapse on my part. But I don't tell her this. I just say, "Don't leave," with tears in my eyes.

She flashes a look in my direction and utters two final words: "Don't cry."

And she's out the door and climbing into the scary aunt's car.

Have fun on your trip.

At that moment, all ties between us were forever dissolved. I never saw the mother again.

CHAPTER NINETEEN

Steve turns left and pulls into the gravel parking lot where a sea of cars confirms what I already know: we're late again. Barbed anxiety envelopes me like a prickly blanket and squabbles with my perpetual anxiety. I hate being late. Never, *ever* be late. The origins of this mandate remain amorphous and unquestioned, vaulted in my rigid, black or white brain. All I know is being late is tantamount to … I don't know what. I just don't like being late.

I mumble, "We'd better hurry," to Steve, who doesn't mind being late at all.

As I maneuver my post-pregnant body out of the minivan, I can hear rock music beating against the walls of the building like it's begging to get out.

Baby number four is cradled in my arms. Steve carries baby number three and numbers one and two walk beside us.

The fusion of dank building and squeezed humanity throws my sensitive olfactory into overdrive. I swallow and ignore the rising nausea as we make our way into the aging Grange Hall that courageously poses as a holding tank for church-goers on Sunday mornings.

It's crowded. Those who got here *on time* have claimed the chairs in the main seating area, but they're standing now, taking their cues from the energetic guitar player up front, singing, clapping, and praising the Lord. The less bubbly lean against the walls. Some coze with neighbors, some stand solitary, some smile and nod. I allow myself a glimpse back outside, slightly comforted that still more families are arriving. We're not the only ones running late.

It's not easy to navigate this narrow aisle, and for a second I resent the inconvenience and how exhausting it is keeping one eye on my children, the other on my feet. I'm wishing myself invisible, because this is a textbook setting for unraveling. The worst case scenario has occupied my mind for so long it seems routine. It whispers reminders of the tightrope and the ravenous alligators below. Say or do something stupid or crazy and tumble to my death as a profusion of judgmental eyes glare at me. And there I am, humiliated, totally nullifying my goal to be normal and blend in, fuse with this group of "like minded" people so I can belong, share in a united purpose.

At a slight clearing, I glance to the front. The pastor is there, alternately plucking his bass guitar and smiling at his comrades. Then he looks down and pushes a tangle of black cords out the way with his foot. Burly, with a tender face, there is something immediately comforting, even magnetic, about him. But I'm a taciturn minion around people in positions of authority. I want him to notice me and I'm relieved when he doesn't.

Steve ushers us up the steps and off to the side of the main area where The Late are relegated. I drop the diaper bag at my feet, readjust my little one, and force myself to sing along.

It's a new start, I tell myself. A new life. *Another* new life.

I'm scripting, fine-tuning this new role. The props include but aren't limited to a life in the country, home schooling a house full of children, tending a garden, a dog, cats, chickens. I'm feigning near Mennonite "purity," me, a woman of virtue, a "gentle spirit." My "worldly" jeans have been boxed and dropped off at Goodwill and now my closet pays homage to my "modesty." I ascribe to the Proverbs 31 model and reinforce my image by verbalizing that I'm thinking about a Bible study to see what those head coverings are all about.

Rehearse something long enough ….

I will go to great lengths in my search for peace. Certainly this latest strategy will permeate my internal life, the one where anxiety and hollowness grip and plague me. This "living for Jesus" will shine a light on my dark and ugly dream world. It will send a message to the devil and he'll get the picture and see that I'm not worth his time. Then maybe I'll feel like I belong at long last.

There are recurring doubts. I lie in bed and wonder if maybe my latest extreme makeover is a little *too* extreme. Maybe it isn't the healthiest thing for my kids. But eventually I shoo all such thoughts out of my mind.

Occasionally, Steve will voice his own concerns in an effort to steer me back toward middle ground. But I either ignore him or bark rebukes such as, "You need to be more 'godly.' You're the problem, not me."

My attitude infuriates him but he doesn't yell or lose control. His silence falls like a sledgehammer.

The guitar player strums quietly. Hands are raised, eyes are closed. Bodies sway back and forth, a metronome on slow. Many people hum or mumble their intimate praises to the Lord. We wait in a creepy sort of netherworld while an indecipherable drone circles the room. The idea is to let the Holy Spirit fill you. We want the Holy Spirit to lead. If we wait on Him, he'll nudge someone to sing out or "give a word" and the rest will follow. The Holy Spirit is in control.

Our former church in Portland was pretty much the antithesis of this place. That package contained a plethora of stately, tie-clad elders and deacons; lots and lots of ministries; buses that picked up the homebound; a massive and expensive building project; traditional hymns, and a prearranged, predictable Sunday morning service. Although not mandated, it was *strongly encouraged* that children attend their age-appropriate Sunday school, an urging that tormented me. What? My children are my most precious possessions. You want me to leave them with a stranger?

I couldn't really enjoy that church. Not with my internal "what if" tape playing endlessly. Day and night it would torment me with a bevy of horrific scenarios involving my children.

Now we're in a church that echoes our convictions, applauding and endorsing the importance of the traditional family worshipping together.

It's only been a few minutes but it seems longer. Eyes are still closed and each member murmurs their personal chant while intervals of a sluggish, barely recognizable worship tune issue from the guitar going solo, presumably to perpetuate the worship state of mind.

Suddenly, "Amazing grace how sweet the sound …" skewers the netherworld. It originates from a woman near the back row. On cue, the group chimes in. The guitar player strums. The bass player plucks. The drummer beats.

And then the pastor preaches. And I come away with a fresh light shining on my glaring flaws and how I need to "get right with God."

He wasn't talking to me. He hardly even looked over at The Late Section. He was speaking in generalities. This is what Steve would say if I voiced to him my feelings.

Oh, these *feelings.* I'm just not myself anymore. But when have I *ever* been myself?

With the arrival of my fourth baby the frustrated curiosities about my childhood came back; my baby years, the mommy ponderings. Maybe it's a hormone thing. About all I can do is hold on to the tidbits I was privy to. Anything more is an unattainable luxury. The mother's interests lie elsewhere.

***

Our gravel driveway is steepest at the end where, after a pair of hairpin turns, it ascends to a clearing and forms a large loop for easy turn around. In the center are four gigantic Douglas firs with a lush ivy grove skirting their trunks.

Steve pulls into the garage and shuts off the engine. We pile out and I inhale the chilly, forest-infused air as I reach down to nuzzle our two cats that appeared from the loft above the garage.

Rising, my pantyhose lose their grip and droop. Hiking them up is futile because I'm between sizes, patiently laboring to rid myself of my post-pregnancy lumps and bumps.

The familiar surroundings induce a relaxed state that I know will last only until the hunger alarm goes off, which it will at any moment.

As I did last week and the week before, I regret that I didn't prepare something before we left for church this morning. How nice it would be to come home to the comforting aroma of a steaming crock pot or a savory-smelling oven. How nice it would be if I provided this for my family, for myself.

But I wasn't hungry this morning before we left. I had the time but I talked myself out of it, like I did last week and the week before. I'm unable to see beyond the right now. Planning things—anything—induces a fresh surge of anxiety and dread that I just don't have the energy to rise above. And so until the demand is in front of me and there is no denying its immediacy, I put it off—whatever "it" might be.

Truth be told, I'm not much of a cook. I rely heavily on a freezer or lazy Susan stocked with Costco's conveniences. I tell myself I'll get more organized once I can get uninterrupted sleep.

Steve holds the baby, who is on the verge of a meltdown of her own as I open a can of refried beans. Burritos again.

The peer pressure is palpable. Steve tells me I shouldn't compare myself with other women and he's right, but I do it anyway, conceding to the familiar voice of self-condemnation.

There are a bevy of Julia Childs and Martha Stewarts at the church to reinforce my domestic struggles. I watch these women, some of them friends now, and wonder how they do it all. Babies, family, home school, the whole bit. They seem so good at all of it, so natural and genuine. For me it's not natural at all and any claim of success is due to sheer determination not any kind of gifting. But these Julias and Marthas are undeniably gifted. From my vantage point—a very limited one, Steve reminds me—they effortlessly cook, teach, and birth babies in the middle of the rice paddy and keep right on working.

I'd like to make this life work. I know my intensions are in the right place: Family First.

***

Our house was built upon a small clearing on a ten acre parcel of Oregon forest. With lots of trails to roam, the anxiety of trespassing is nil and there is an unmistakable freedom here that can't exist on a city lot. Past the pump house, the topography gently descends to a small lake, surrounded on all sides by hills and pointy tree tops. We see ducks, geese, beaver, frogs. There is rumored to be roaming cougar and bear but all we see are deer. Sometimes a party of six will wander through and nibble on my struggling roses and strawberry plants.

We moved here during the pinnacle of summer. How easy it was to embrace my verdant surroundings. I'd feel almost giddy and childlike, communing with nature as I did so long ago and affording my children the same opportunity.

With the onset of autumn and the disappearance of blue sky and sunshine, I find myself with a compulsive need to weather watch, propelled by what feels like a powerless childlike vulnerability. Often, I'll catch myself standing at the living room window, unsure how long I've been there, gazing out at the towering tree tops swaying in the wind. Other times I'm staring out the kitchen window, reading the thermometer mounted to a nearby post, wondering if freezing weather is imminent.

On some insecure level of my being, I believe that my fate and the fate of my loved ones is somehow linked to the mercy of the weather. Nestled here in the nucleus of nature and its imposing crown jewels, I'm compelled to stay hypervigilant, diligently attuned to the skies—just in case one of those jewels happens to disengage and uproot from its setting.

How long will this forest stay vertical? Both awake and asleep, I keep visualizing trees crashing down on the house.

My anxiety has more intense ventures as well. It takes its cues from some arcane force that's been with me for decades. It has upped the ante, heaving a continuous projection of morbid bloodletting on my psyche. It operates without my consent; a reel without an off switch, replaying a deplorable anti-story without beginning, plot or end.

I don't know why my mind is doing this to me. I must be demon possessed. How can I be a Christian and think these kinds of things? What would the church ladies think? I love my children more than life itself and I'm so afraid for their safety. If I continue to keep this a secret, will things get worse? Am I capable of making this slasher film a reality?

My postpartum recovery seems mysteriously impeded, stymied. It's taken me to a new low emotionally and physically. I'm tense and snap at the slightest provocation. And I'm still bleeding. I should be done by now. My hair is falling out in clumps and sometimes a strand will wrap itself tightly around my baby's finger or toe. I panic because I'm sure the hair will squeeze and slice her tender skin and cut off circulation and ultimately she'll lose the digit completely.

I can't let myself believe that I'm losing my mind so I just stay busy mothering, perpetuating my double life.

**

It's comical how my pervasive skepticism has proven erroneous once again. Maybe it was just wishful thinking, since I'm not terribly fond of snow, or, more accurately, the inconveniences that snow-laden roads cause. But there it is, blanketing everything, with no end in sight as more downy flakes fall like placid feathers, adding to the already record-breaking winter wonderland.

I step out, just for a second. I'd like to absorb the hush, the stillness and serenity, bottle it and hoard it to sip slowly to fuel some kind of inner peace. I take a deep breath of winter and wood smoke.

Serenity is no match for my paranoia. The silence is eerie, uncomfortably quiet, like a weighty force that renders my ears useless. When my ears hear nothing, I am alerted to my pervasive internal nothingness. Too much silence is deafening.

I'm startled by the ominous, echoic splintering and splitting of Douglas fir flesh. An upper branch on a nearby tree has collapsed under the weight of the snow, followed by a cloud of white. Now that I think of it, I've been hearing intermittent vestiges of this since I woke up. But out here, the volume is on ten, which is code for earsplitting. Another branch splinters over by the pump house, and another off in the distance. Silence. Eerie momentary silence. And then another crack and split up high, followed by the hiss of falling snow. All of the branch casualties are victims of the heavy, overnight snowfall. For reasons that I can't begin to understand, the sound of tree branches splitting is pummeling me into panic overdrive. Something bad is happening.

Back inside, I head straight for the woodstove to warm my hands and try again to make sense of my internal chaos. But there's no time for that now.

With the troops properly donned for the winter wonderland, we tromp through the knee-high powder to the driveway that in short order will become a makeshift toboggan run.

The trees continue to splinter and snap and I labor to tune out their agony. Rationally, I know what's happening, but logic doesn't comfort me. Neither does the reality that I will continue to hear this until the snow melts. I'm so afraid!

I won't let myself think about how close I am to the edge.

***

In another month, my fall over that edge will be a bitter reality.

***

In earthquake-prone areas, citizens stay on the alert, at least to some extent. Drills are rehearsed and tactical emergency strategies are at the ready so no one needs to panic. Earthquakes are a natural phenomenon and there is nothing mystical or hocus-pocus to be concerned with.

I *don't* live in an earthquake-prone area. Quite the opposite. But hidden in some psychic, foggy corner, a replay continues its decades-long sequence. *Me and my Hawaiian classmates … racing to the door … the deafening freight train…*

So when the predawn hours on that March day usher in the same freight train, no time has passed at all.

CHAPTER TWENTY

A layer of foam shimmies across the sand. In the distance I see a few moving dots but other than that the beach is deserted. It's April and it's cold. Not exactly the best weather for a coastal getaway but I didn't want to disappoint Steve and the kids. They were really looking forward to spending time with our church friends.

It's been a whole month since the 5.5 earthquake shocked me to my core. I should probably be over it by now, but I'm not. I can't seem to function. Like an out-of-control merry-go-round, my mind keeps replaying the same terror-filled event, over and over.

Earlier, at lunch, Kaitlin, a church-friend, cast me a concerned looked and I realized my distress was leaking out. *My image, my dying image.*

"You should go see this guy who does deliverance," she said, without knowing even a fraction of my story. "He's like a miracle worker."

Her ensuing litany of justifications didn't quite pierce the fog surrounding my brain.

"He's been counseling couples and casting out demons. Everyone seems to be doing better after working with him."

She thinks I'm possessed by a demon.

I muttered, "I need to think about it." Then I got up and walked down to the beach.

Actually, I had been thinking about it long before Kaitlin's suggestion. I'd seen him from a distance, at church with his bevy of followers all waiting, I assumed, for their chance at deliverance. There was something both appealing and frightening about his essence. I wasn't sure if he'd be able to help me, but I was pretty sure I was demon possessed. There was no other conceivable way to explain my horrendous feelings of panic, my dreams, the bloody, violent images running through my mind. My anxiety has been intense for a long time, but since the earthquake it's become unbearable.

Salty gusts pummel my face and force me to turn away from the misty horizon. I can see glimpses of the beautiful three story beach house behind a cluster of coastal pines. Its roof is pointy, nearly vertical, with a vast number of windows that afford exceptional views of the ocean. My family's bedrooms are on the third floor—too far from an exit. Last night, I lay paralyzed, waiting for something terrible to happen.

I think of the shelf of unaccommodating self-help books back home. They all allude to persistent adult conflicts being a carry-over from childhood. In my case, having a violent father and a dismissive mother wasn't exactly idyllic. I wonder how much of what I am dealing with now is because of my history.

I turn my fidgety body back toward the ocean, allowing the icy wind to punish me. I'm continually on edge. *Hypervigilant*, the books call it. I want to die, because I'm so tired and death feels like the only way to quiet the stream of ill-fated missives thundering through my head.

But dying isn't an option.

Oddly, I feel a subtle resoluteness here on the beach as I mull over my friend's suggestion. It's as if her words have served as a permission of sorts, a validation. I think I'm ready to approach this miracle worker guy.

***

I'm pretty sure that I will be much more of a challenge for Brock than he's used to. From what I've gathered, his clientele consist mostly of regular church-going people with squeaky clean histories seeking a spiritual tune-up rather than an overhaul, people blissfully ignorant of life on the dirty side of the train tracks. No, I'm pretty sure Brock will have his hands full with this "client" or whatever he calls those who seek his help.

It isn't until Steve maneuvers the car around that last bend and the modest ranch house comes in to view that my anxiety really kicks in. *What am I doing this for? Seeking help from a complete stranger? What am I thinking?* Now that we've arrived, it's difficult to fight the compulsion to forget the whole thing, turn the car around and head home.

Steve parks the car under a weeping willow. As its leafy stems dance to the slight breeze, I continue to minimize my troubles, chastising myself for always being so impetuous, jumping without calculating the distance, diving in with little respect for the undercurrents and where they might take me.

Following Steve's tentative knock, a fifty-something-looking man opens the door. Our eyes meet briefly before my shame forces me to look away. I've always prided myself on eschewing current fads and yet here I am, in the midst of the latest and greatest without having to elbow my way to the front. Strange.

He's more intimidating up close. Although not a tall man, he carries himself with a slightly self-aggrandizing stance. *Or is it just my imagination?* Is it his colossal, effusive presence or my pathetic need? On the one hand it feels liberating to stand up, stretch and discard my stockpile of pretenses, but it's also unnerving as hell.

He ushers us to his modest living room where a picture window frames a pastoral green carpet that stretches for maybe a quarter of a mile before abutting a busy highway. Above it, the sky is bold and far-reaching, unencumbered by the tall Douglas firs of home. On a sunny day, I'm sure it's beautiful. But today it's an ashen, nondescript canopy, silent, as if waiting for an impending storm.

Brock sits down and sets the telephone on the coffee table in front of us. He sighs, stares at me for a minute, and I conclude that Steve and I must be intruding. He crosses one leg over the other and, with full inflection, launches into his gritty frustration with the modern-day church. This immediately appeals to my fringe thinking. Later I'll learn that this is his way, charging ahead with his opinions in an effort to either influence people or get them to object and force a debate.

Steve is not a debater. He fidgets a bit with his hands and nods, looking for points of agreement while I study the landscape outside the picture window.

"The church is steeped in fear. All the rules and bylaws, they're designed to keep people enslaved out of fear. Legalism is fear. Christians don't need to live that way. Jesus came to set the captives free. I'm an expert on fear, having grown up with it, but once I realized I didn't have to live that way any longer, I let it go. Why aren't we seeing churches preach freedom? Because churches love their legalism, that's why."

The phone rings and Brock picks it up, rises, and saunters toward the kitchen where his vociferation reveals the nature of his call. During ensuing sessions these interruptions will incite a raging jealousy that can only be calmed by reminding myself that, unlike the unfortunate caller, I'm *here* in Brock's presence. She's not. But on this first visit, I'm ignorant of the internal skirmishes to come.

Next to the window, Brock's wife is seated in what is obviously *her* chair. She goes from reading the newspaper to working on a cross-stitch project under the light of a lamp beside her. Pillow cases for a relative who's getting married in a few weeks, she tells us. I wonder what it must be like for her to have a constant stream of needy women darkening her door. Later I'll learn that she is the archetypal stand-by-her-man wife, a pillar of hospitality with the patience of a saint.

Brock returns, sets the phone down exactly as before. Like an appendage, he keeps it at his side, always anticipating its summons. I ignore his divided attention out of politeness and because I already feel some kind of indebtedness toward him.

"Like I said, churches today don't even realize how legalistic they are. They've got all these rules about tithing, for instance. But tithing is an Old-Testament mandate ...."

Eventually, either satisfied that he's gotten everything off his chest or else detecting my impatience, Brock tables his diatribe, leans forward, looks directly at me and asks, "So, what are you afraid of?"

Stifling a burst of resentment over his brash intrusion, I swallow, take a deep breath and begin my confession. "Um, well, I'm afraid of everything," I mumble, avoiding eye contact by staring at my sweaty hands. "I feel like something bad is going to happen all the time. And sometimes I can actually see it happening in my mind, like the car going off the road or the house crumbling on top me. Plus I have these really grotesque images of my cutting and torturing people, especially my kids." With that, I quickly glance at him, feeling an infinitesimal sense of release, as if this small admission of a breach in my sanity has in some obscure way begun to heal it.

The phone rings again, and, while Brock is out of the room, I begin making a list of all the things I'm afraid of, mostly moving things such as, cars, trains, buses ….

With an outstretched hand, Brock says, "Let me see what you wrote down."

I hand him the list.

"I've never seen anyone with this much fear. You're pretty bad off."

I'm not sure how to handle this information. It feels good to be listened to but I can't really tell if he's validating or insulting me. But there's no doubt that, on some level, I relish being the object of his focus.

Steve, seated beside me, squeezes my hand while Brock speaks with unmitigated authority on what the Bible has to say on the subject of demons, spiritual warfare, and fear.

"No Christian should be tormented by evil spirits. Jesus Christ defeated Satan on the cross. Do you believe that?"

I nod and secretly wonder if Brock is implying that I'm suffering because of my lack of faith, that if I truly believed that demons had no right to be plaguing me, they wouldn't be, and that it's my fault I'm so "bad off."

Brock makes it clear. "You need to trust me and believe what I tell you. Do you submit to the authority of Jesus Christ?"

"Yes," I say, not really understanding what exactly *the authority of Jesus Christ* is.

"Are you willing to do whatever it takes?"

I look at Steve, then back at Brock. "Yes." Obviously, this is what I'm supposed to say.

"What do you remember about your family?"

"My parents got divorced when I was nine. My dad was angry and physically abusive. My mom was distant and uncaring. My parents didn't like kids."

"What do you remember about your grandparents?"

"My mom's father died when I was living in Hawaii. I don't remember too much about him, just riding in his car … I don't remember where we went, though."

Unlike professional therapists who keep their assumptions to themselves, Brock nods, smiles and states emphatically, "Your grandfather took you places and molested you. Was he a Mason?"

"I think so." I struggle to recall images of his home so long ago. I blurt, "I remember his red hat. I wasn't supposed to touch it." I haven't thought about that red hat in years. It was my grandmother who was so adamant that I not touch the thing.

"A *fez*. All the Shriners wore them. This means he was a probably a 33rd degree Mason."

Apparently this is supposed to mean something, but I just shrug my shoulders, glance quickly at Steve and then back at Brock.

"Freemasonry, like other secret societies, looks like a humanitarian organization from the outside, but that's just a front. What goes on inside is bad stuff. The role of their highest members is to design and implement a world takeover. Those people they abuse as kids are the pawns they'll use to usher in The New World Order. They get programmed to respond and obey." Brock seems to know what he's talking about. Not only is he adept at understanding the Bible, he knows all about modern-day events and how they're leading up to the second coming of Christ. He understands how the various secret societies are involved and how the common, everyday people will be fooled by the devil into doing his bidding. Could I be sitting in the presence of greatness? I'm starting to think I am.

As if sensing how impressed I am, Brock pauses and looks at me. His diagnosis is straightforward. "Your grandfather took you to the Lodge and abused you with sodomy and communion. This was to install demons and enslave you, keep you childish and under Masonic control. Even though you're now an adult, you can still be accessed with the brainwashing they did when you were little."

Something about Brock's simple but tender prayer, "Lord protect her," works magic. Although the full implications aren't immediately noticed, his words unwittingly unseal a long-forgotten vault where my own childish vulnerabilities have been sequestered for decades. Like a magnet, Brock's fatherly compassion gently calls the little child out of the depths of hibernation. But I hide that part of me and follow his lead.

When Brock is satisfied that I believe his diagnosis, he leans forward in his chair.

"Take my hand."

Obeying without hesitation, I reach over and grip his hand.

"Now, look in my eyes."

This is much more difficult. I want to look away. I've never been good with eye contact, especially with men.

"Now, tell me the first thing that comes to you."

I nod, my eyes burning.

"Spirit of her grandfather," Brock states, looking directly into my soul, "I command you by the authority of Jesus Christ to tell me your name."

"I hear the name of my grandfather."

"Did you enter her through sex abuse when she was a baby?"

"Yes." I don't know whether it's me or this demon thinking or talking. I push aside my disorientation and comply.

"What is your purpose?"

Silence. I shake my head.

"I command you to tell me why you entered her," Brock has raised his voice. He's angry. Or is he? I look away.

"Look at me, Grace. Demon of sodomy, I command you to tell me what your purpose is."

"Control," I mutter, fighting to avoid eye contact with Brock.

"Is it true that your purpose is to control her with fear? Keep her enslaved to her grandfather's wishes?"

"Yes." I still don't know if it's me or the demon talking.

"Are you defeated?"

"Yes."

"Then I command you by the authority of Jesus Christ to take all your underlings and go to the pit of hell."

Brock pauses for a few seconds, releases my hand and asks, "Did it leave?"

"I think so," I say, trying to sound confident but feeling fuzzy and embarrassed. I can tell his wife is getting sleepy.

The clock wraps up its series of chimes but Brock ignores them, sits back in his chair and says nothing. His penetrating eyes observe my movements. I can't look at him for more than a few seconds at a time. Befuddled over everything that has transpired today, I finally summon the wherewithal to offer a meek, "Thank you."

He smiles briefly, looks at Steve and says, "I'm amazed at how many people are coming to me who've been abused by the Masons."

Steve nods.

***

On the drive home, I'm in a fatigued daze. It's a lot to take in, Brock's version of my history. My grandfather and his participation in a secret society? It all seems so crazy and far-fetched. Yet it has a certain twisted appeal, too, and I can't deny a certain fascination with the idea of being inducted into a secret society. It means I wasn't ignored after all. I was important. Being abused for a cause, even a diabolical one, is infinitely more appealing than being completely ignored. I'm feeling better about this new version of my history, even if I don't remember it. *But why don't I remember it?*

According to Brock, the brainwashing that was done to me as a kid was still active in my brain.. Even as an adult I've been as vulnerable as a helpless child.

And the idea that I could still be *accessed* by "them"? The elusive *them*?

Who are these people? Do I interact with them every day? Are they really good liars, people with ulterior motives? Church people? Homeschoolers? People at the store? How can I know the people I'm vulnerable to? Or maybe I'm no longer vulnerable now that the demon of my grandfather has been cast out. *Was it cast out?*

Even before the next day, my mind is back in doom territory. I can't sleep. My mind keeps seeing horrific images. Statues, at first snow white, are burned black as midnight. They fall on me and I jump, startled by something that isn't there.

***

It's a late April morning, still winter cold, but I can't close my front door because the trapped feeling is overwhelming. I've got to be able to get outside quickly where nothing will fall on me and no one will sneak up on me. I keep thinking about the wide open space surrounding Brock's home.

I cry. I pray. I'm disoriented and my head feels warm, like the blood in my system is circulating so fast I'm going to explode. "God, if Brock is right and I really was abused by my grandpa, please give me a confirmation."

While my younger kids are napping, I enlist the older two to take charge while I make my way up to the loft in the garage where old boxes are kept. Thumbing through an aging family album, the tiniest corner of a small photo tucked behind a bigger one peeks out at me as if its long-awaited discovery has been appointed for this very hour. I grab it, pull it out, and bring it under the light. My grandfather, circa 1960, is lazing in a chair. A Masonic newspaper is in his lap.

Ah-ha. My grandfather really was a Mason. This photo confirms it. It's the *sign* I've been asking for, God's confirmation that Brock is right. I'm sure of it.

Back in the house, I contemplate whether discovering this photo is a good enough reason to call Brock. I don't want to intrude. I'm sure he's got more important things to do than listen to my drivel. But I want— *need*—to hear his voice. The more I try to talk myself out it, the stronger the impulse to call him becomes.

I grab the phone and dial.

"Hi, Brock? This is Grace. I, um, wanted to let you know that I found a picture of my grandfather and he really *was* a Mason."

Brock is in a good mood and, despite my nervous stuttering, seems genuinely pleased to hear from me. The needle has released its complicated elixir and Brock's essence flows freely through my bloodstream. I'm calm. Actually, I'm giddy.

"I want you to have nothing to do with your relatives. They might try to lure you back into their version of the facts," Brock commands with an air of confident authority.

"Okay," I say, having already eliminated most of them from my life anyway. I can't let myself think about how much I'm hurting Sarah and Anna.

Wrapping up our phone call, I confess, "I'm still really anxious and I keep seeing images of cutting and violence, especially of me cutting my kids."

"We didn't get to the bottom of it," he states without hesitation.

There's more? The exhilaration I feel at picturing myself back in Brock's living room for another go around is reason enough to have any demon. Soon, when Brock has time, he assures me, I'll resume my rightful place at the feet of the one anointed by God.

CHAPTER TWENTY-ONE

Through the ensuing months, I learn more about Brock and his ministry. A part-time calling, he fits his deliverance sessions into his schedule when he can, but because he's in such high demand, it can be weeks or even months between them. To fill the gap, he uses the telephone quite liberally.

There are periods when he'll call me daily to remind me to stay focused on Jesus.

Other times I can go days without hearing his voice. It's these times when I wonder what's going on. Have I been abandoned? Dropped to the bottom of the pile? I'm still struggling with intense anxiety. Why didn't that demon leave when Brock commanded it to? Why won't God heal me? Why can't Brock tell me what's going on? The uncertainty of not knowing my status with Brock is agonizing and because I'm so mentally tormented, it's too easy to assume the worst. *He hates me.*

What I really need is consistency, but I don't know how to articulate that. Or maybe I don't know what I need.

Brock is unrelenting in his search for answers as to why the demon won't leave me. He's completely convinced that I'm suffering needlessly at the hands of some stalwart, stubborn fiend. Not only does he study the Bible and other relevant books, he also extracts information from the evil entities themselves that inhabit the victims of the Freemasons. All of this "detective work," as he calls it, means I can rest assured that eventually Brock will discover the offending demon's identity and it will be forced to release me from its grip.

I wish I could just sit back and wait, quietly trust that Brock will keep his promise to me. But trust and acute anxiety don't generally go well together.

***

Tonight, Brock has time to see me.

Driving to his house, alone this time, my anxiety rises dramatically as I round the last corner before turning onto his lane. It's the demons in me, agitated over their impending exposure. I've got to ignore the resistance. "Kick it in the teeth," Brock commands later after I reveal it to him. At first I think he's joking, but maybe not.

Brock details his latest theories. "A demon will lose its power when we know its identity and how it entered. Demons don't like being exposed," he says with an air confidence that silences any thought of contradiction. "Demons cling to a person's deceit. People believe the lies they've been told. It's the truth that sets people free. Demons have no power over the truth."

On the first session, Brock was sure the demon's name was the same as my grandfather's. The next time it was "Satan," then "Baal," then "Beelzebub," then "Master Controller." Then it was "Druid." Then I lost track.

"You work for Lucifer," Brock says, looking into my stinging eyes. "Are you the kingpin?"

"Yes," I say, ringing my agitated hands.

"Admit that you entered her at three years of age and that you have no power over her."

"No. I have a right to stay."

Defiant demons are Brock's specialty. "Look me in the eyes," he demands, perching himself in front of me and holding my arms to my sides.

I look at him but the line has blurred. I'm not sure if it's me or the demon Brock is talking to. My eyes burn. *Is the demon making my eyes burn? Can demons do that?*

"Turn off the lights." I demand back, trying to break free of Brock's grip on my arms.

Brock's voice goes low, gravelly. He jerks my arms tighter and says, "I don't take orders from demons. Now I command you in the name of the Lord Jesus Christ to tell me what your name is."

Because I don't answer, Brock launches into his leading questions. "Did you enter her at three years of age?"

"Yes."

"Was it a sodomy ritual?"

"Yes."

"What is your name?"

"Lucifer," I say.

"Are you defeated and ready to go to the pit?"

I might answer either way. If I say yes, Brock will follow with, "I command you by the authority of Jesus Christ to go to the pit of hell and take all your underlings with you."

If I say no, he'll say, "Do you want it to go, Grace?"

"Yes," I reply.

"Brock?" A soft voice on the opposite side of the room interrupts my agitation. "Maybe she needs to renounce the oaths."

"Marge, you don't know what you're talking about," Brock snarls at her.

Marge offers a weak smile and, turtle-like, retreats inside her shell. I can tell she'd like a chance to explain herself, but Brock won't allow it.

"You people all think too much," Brock says. "That's not where I'm going with this, Marge."

I offer Marge an empathic smile, hoping it conveys my condolences over her husband's egregious overuse of the dreaded accusatory *you* statements.

"Some people don't like my sarcasm," he says later, over the meal Marge has lovingly prepared. Perhaps his wry grin is intended to absolve him of any wrongdoing.

"Well, your sarcasm is mild compared to what I had to endure," I offer. I'm keenly aware that by minimizing Brock's caustic tongue I'm just enabling him, but confronting him is not an option. Tempting as it might be, telling him to rot in hell and then walking out the door would hurt me a lot worse than it would hurt him. And it would jeopardize my healing.

The clock begins its late-night chimes. It's time for me to go. Despite feeling guilty for taking so much of Brock's time, I want to stay and bask in his presence. There is something inexplicably alluring about him.

Brock's wife has nodded off. Her breathing is heavy and her head is down, turned to one side. She looks uncomfortable in her chair on the other side of the room.

Brock notices me looking at her and follows my gaze. He looks back at me and smiles. His tender feelings for her just add to his enigma. He obviously loves her, but he sure doesn't hesitate to bite her head off when he's frustrated. I have trouble comprehending this blatant dichotomy.

There is a special kind of warmth that peeks out of him at certain times but it can't seem to overrule his usual no-nonsense demeanor. This man of God who professes his allegiance to the heavenly father, who has the "gift of discernment" alluded to in the Bible, defies my preconceived stereotypes. Perhaps that's the reason I'm so enamored. Maybe it's his bad-ass attitude that appeals to me.

At twilight, Marge pulled the drapes, closing off the fading landscape. I wanted to protest but thought better of it. Now, the late-evening room is cozy with lamplight. Something in the back of my being reminds me that I'm a fairly decent-looking woman and, if I tried, I could probably seduce this man who has so effortlessly completely hijacked my fucked up psyche.

Something keeps that woman in me from emerging, undoing my blouse, straddling his lap and kissing his neck. I can't sabotage my relationship with Brock. It's the child in me who loves him, I remind myself, not the woman. But the woman wants him. Or does she? Yes, I think she does.

Brock's wife would wake up, I remind her.

There is silence between us. Brock is sleepy. I take this as my cue to gather my stuff and leave.

Driving home, I have time to mull over this complicated, shameful relationship I have forged with Brock. Unabashedly trampling its sacredness, I swing open the forbidden door and inhabit the dark woman.

I wonder if he wants me, if those mysterious looks he sends my way are really something much more than fatherly concern. Maybe he secretly wishes he could get me alone and take his work-worn hands and touch me. If it should happen, if he were to give even the slightest indication that he wanted me, I'd willingly and willfully comply. Summoning my passions, I would lead his hands to forbidden places and he would feel every inch of me.

I shiver at the thought of it. Just stay on the road Grace, you *whore*.

***

A few weeks later, Brock declares that I have Multiple Personality Disorder. "A child mindset," he tells me. It feels like an indictment. But it also fuels my desire to be important, special, to rewrite the years of childhood neglect into something exceptional.

Brock reads about MPD in a book written by a Christian psychologist. He takes the book's recovery approach quite literally, wanting to talk to all my "personalities." Following the remedy laid out in the book, I dutifully comply, "mapping" and naming my different selves, trying to gain an understanding of their unique characteristics.

Multiple personalities by traumatic dissociation makes a lot of sense. It explains why I don't remember the Masonic rituals. It explains why I'm so ambivalent all the time, never adhering to one set of values. It explains the slutty me, the girl who wants to break all the rules with Brock. It explains the good girl me, who wants Brock's approval and friendship. It explains the child me who wants a daddy and why a part of me hates Brock's guts and wants nothing to do with him.

My commitment to studying my multiple personality nuances swallows up a lot of time that I would otherwise spend feeling anxious and abandoned. I feel productive and empowered, like I'm working toward a solution to my anxiety, my freedom. But it doesn't eliminate this horrendous ache in my gut. Instead, it's as if my emotional devastation is what's keeping me alive.

***

Steve is awake, moving around the bedroom, probably getting ready for work. I raise my head just long enough to see the clock. It's definitely morning. *Damn. Why didn't I just die in my sleep?*

As he grabs his keys, he asks, "Will you be able to handle things today?" He doesn't attempt to hide his irritation with me.

"Yes," I mutter in the bitchiest tone I can muster.

I roll over and hide myself under the covers as he leaves the room.

He's such a freaking bastard lately. All he cares about is himself. I hate his guts.

Once he's gone, I roll myself back and grab the pad of paper on the nightstand. The flashbacks that occurred during the night are scribbled across several pages. I call them flashbacks but I don't know if that's what they really are. They seem familiar on one level but completely and utterly foreign on another, like I'm looking through someone else's eyes in real-time. It's bizarre. Sometimes I'll remember the specifics, but, just as often, within seconds of it occurring, it will be completely erased from my consciousness. If I'm quick, I'll get it scribbled on paper before it is gone.

A gold dagger. I don't remember seeing this.

Pandora's Box. I do remember this. It was a dimly-lit, cave-like room and someone opened a large box and a bunch of black things flew out of it. It was like seeing a movie.

Baby, monkey, kitty … drowning in the sink … brown stuff. Oh, yes, I remember seeing that. I felt it, too. I was holding a baby under water. Or was it a monkey? She went limp and brown stuff came out of her mouth and her eyes bulged. This reminds me of the earlier, terrifying flashback where it was *me* under the water, drowning. I could feel the terror of not being able to breathe. I came up and corn was in my mouth and no matter how much I tried to spit it out, I couldn't.

I sigh and wonder if last night's flashbacks—or whatever they might be—could be considered worthy enough to warrant a telephone call to Brock. I need to hear his voice.

I sigh and turn over, push my face into the pillow wishing I could smother myself to death. I want to stop breathing, I hurt so bad.

My need for Brock has grown exponentially over the past few months. It's like a mysterious void in my gut, a missing ingredient in my DNA. It's as if my life force has been sucked out of me, leaving me swirling in a painful empty vortex. It's an inner vacancy that centers on Brock and my need for him. I can't satisfy it any other way. I need to hear his voice. , But I need a good reason to call him, I remind myself, taking a breath, rolling over yet again and looking at scribbled flashback notes. Is there anything here worthy of making a call?

I don't want to intrude. He's already sick of me.

I'm reminded of a recent call to Brock. I don't know what he was doing but whatever it was, it was obvious he didn't like the interruption.

His terse, dismissive side was fully evident and even though he'd earlier assured me that it was okay to call him, clearly, this time, it wasn't.

I can't predict if Brock will help me or just offer me some stupid advice like, "Read your Bible. Focus on Jesus" which is just code for, "I'm too busy for you right now and you annoy the hell out of me."

I despise my neediness; the urge to cut myself is almost unbearable.

Sitting up in bed, I see through the opened closet door my retired jumper dresses. Damn. What was I thinking, assuming my modest dress code could deliver me from the evil that courses through my veins? It was after one of Brock's diatribes on legalism that I looked down at my jumper and wondered if maybe in my zeal for "righteousness" I had become the queen of legalism.

In contrast to the jumpers hanging neatly in the closet, my new jeans are lazily thrown over the chair. My new persona is more liberal and wears jeans and likes men to notice her. Paramount is the approval I'll receive from Brock. But my motives are complicated and the loose-fitting jumper-wearing me, legalistic to a fault, keeps chastising the seductress-me for her affinity for body-hugging denim.

As I go about my mothering, Brock is stationed above my left shoulder, hovering, observing my day to day comings and goings. Silently, I talk to him. He watches, also silent. His presence helps me deal with the horrific pain of abandonment.

When Brock's virtual presence isn't enough and feelings ovwhelm me, my system sends the screaming message for more. I switch personalities, becoming a crazed lunatic, an addict—and Brock is my drug. Desperation annihilates every other aspect of my life. *I need Brock. I'd kill for him.*

Although on some far-removed pragmatic level, I know my feelings of abandonment come from my childhood, it is a very real and present energy that sucks the life out of me.

***

"Hi, Marge, is Brock there?" I say, desperate, ashamed, and struggling to sound remotely polite.

"Uh, we've got someone here today. He'll have to call you back."

"Okay." I sigh, stuffing my anguish into some kind of mental storage facility. I summon my manners just long enough to say goodbye. I don't want to know who that someone is. I just want all of this to go away. *Shit.*

Despite the threat of rain, I don my running shoes. Leaving my son in charge and ignoring my fear of an earthquake, I head outside where I can race around the driveway's turnaround loop and let go of my pent-up rage. It's no more than an eighth of a mile, but it serves its purpose, providing the predictable consistency that is otherwise missing from my healing journey.

I must not need Brock or his help, I conclude as the threat of rainfall grows more persuasive. I mean, the Bible says that God promises to supply all our needs. If my needs aren't being met, then what I *think* are needs must not be. The Bible doesn't lie, so it must be *me* who's off, *me* who thinks I need something I don't.

The ache in my gut forces me to stop, bend, and breathe deep. I've been forgotten by God. That is the only thing that makes sense.

"What terrible thing have I done that you have to punish me so severely, God?" I yell up to the ashen sky.

Disenchantment, anguish, feelings of utter aloneness course through my veins while I continue around the loop, walking now.

Shit, what am I thinking? What I'm suffering is nothing like what Jesus suffered. I'm such a freaking wuss. I've got to stop whining to God about every little thing.

***

The window rattles. Adrenaline surges. The desire to bolt from my seat on the sofa and out the door is instantaneous, but I sit, frozen, listening, waiting.

Nothing more. I can relax. *Damn aftershocks.* The deafening sound of the freight train still haunts me when my world is quiet. And when my world is noisy, I hear, just beyond the din, the screams of tortured children. Lately it's all I can do to use the vacuum. I'm constantly turning it off and listening to reassure myself that my kids are fine.

I readjust my legs under me and grab my notebook and pencil. After Brock decided that the Christian psychologist's book on MPD was too complicated, I had to nix my "mapping" exercise and figure out some other way to empower myself. That whole personality thing felt iffy anyway. On the one hand, it seemed like a logical way to explain my constantly fluctuating opinions. But I didn't have the typical MPD symptom of losing time. Still, there are instances when I think Brock is wrong and that I am *a multiple,* as the book says, but I have to keep this to myself. Brock will just rebuff my comment and tell me I've got a "child mindset" which sends me into a rage.

Brock forbids me to read *any* self-help book. "Those books program you to believe that healing is a long, drawn-out process, when it isn't."

I've taken to drawing pictures of some of my flashbacks. Once completed, I send them in the mail to Brock. It makes me feel closer to him. Besides, he much prefers my pictures over the angry letters he receives after he's pissed me off with his "Read your Bible" bullshit.

Today I'm going to draw the cave where the dim light casts a glow on Pandora's Box.

As I work this image from a quick flash into a lasting rendition, my younger kids nap and the older two are outside. It's much easier to let them play now that we're situated on a secluded, forested ten-acre lot. People hardly ever come up our steep driveway and if they do, I can see and hear them before they get here so there is plenty of warning.

My son is over by the garage working with the discarded wood pallets, ripping them apart and rebuilding them into something, I'm not sure what. My daughter is feigning domesticity in the playhouse. They're so good at playing independently. I'm blessed to have them in my life.

I'm so very lucky. There is no doubt about it. So why do I feel so awful? The pain in my gut is horrific and all-consuming. I just want to die.

I work the pencil around the page, summoning my memory for the finer details while alternately wondering what Brock will think of my latest submission. Likely, he'll bring it out like he's done with the earlier drawings and show it to the crowd gathered in his living room for his latest method, "a healing service." He'll tell them it's to illustrate the anguish of the Masonic ritual victims. He relishes one drawing in particular—"The Locked-Up Child"—a pencil rendition of a girl locked in a cage with a key just out of reach. Although the attendees seem compassionate, I feel a strange, convoluted mix of emotions. It's affirming to have people take an interest in my drawings but I feel like a total fraud when they study them. I can't help the feeling that I'm fabricating this entire otherworld and that if they look closely they'll see what a phony, disingenuous person I am.

With baby sounds emanating from the other room, I sigh and toss my work aside for now. I'll take the Littles outside and maybe try a little gardening. I amaze myself with my ability to function while carrying around this much emotional pain, living outside myself, disconnected, robotic. Maybe my abilities are fueled by Brock's constant presence above my left shoulder.

My babies' smiles are contagious. As they absorb the effervescence of childhood I breathe in the outdoors and try to break my brittle shell to allow the joy entrance.

If only people could understand. If only my friends had a clue what terrible agony I feel all the time. I don't blame them. There's no way to adequately feel someone else's pain. On the rare occasion I actually have enough energy to see anyone, I paint a fake smile, sit quietly and listen. I can't make myself vulnerable to them because I don't trust my own instability. It's too easy for me to lose control and fall apart.

***

Months turn into a year, then two, now three. While Brock jaunts through his other obligations, my boiling desperation and resentment make me a bitch to live with. *How dare he get to live his life while I'm hanging off the edge, waiting for him to make time to help me like he promised.*

"Here's a psychologist I'd like you to see. He's been helping me," Steve tells me one morning, setting a card on the nightstand before grabbing his keys and leaving.

A psychologist? But I'd be betraying Brock, wouldn't I?

The turbulence between Steve and me has been on the decline lately. "Brock is ill-equipped to help you deal with all of the emotions you're feeling," he'll gently tell me. "You need to sort them out with a professional."

Like everything else in my life, I'm in a quandary over this. In a way, it would be nice to have someone to talk to. Brock doesn't let me talk. He's not a listener. He's a fixer, a rescuer. And as angry as he makes me sometimes, I do appreciate his efforts. But a real therapist would be a way to get what is missing. He'd let me talk and he'd listen. But thinking about how I would have to teach the therapist all about ritual abuse and hidden memories and recovered memories and multiple personalities, no. I'm just not capable of that.

And, maybe most importantly, I'd have to come face to face with the fact that I'm a fraud.

CHAPTER TWENTY-TWO

Despite my best efforts, the axiom "things have to get worse before they get better" seems to ring true. They will get better, I keep telling myself. I *know* they will. *But when*?

Steve has arranged to get babysitting help. This morning as I lie here in bed, a teenager is pseudo-mothering my children, living my life. I resent it. I love my children. Child noises reach me and I feel a terrible longing to go back to my life. I'm being robbed. I hate this.

***

Occasionally, a visitor will trudge their way up our steep gravel drive. Yesterday it was Donita, but it's always the same whoever it is. I sit silently, trying to smile while they chatter on. I suppose they're trying to get me to think about something other than my misery, but I wish just one of them would stop talking and invite *me* to talk, compel me and genuinely listen without offering pat answers. Unlike them, I can't throw words out and hope someone will catch them. I tried it a few times, but they dropped to the floor and I felt myself shatter into a thousand pieces. I can't risk that happening again. So I remain silent. I smile. I wish I could do more. I can't.

Lying in bed, totally alone, paper and pen are my therapy. I write. Reams and reams of writings fill a box in the corner of the room. Not just my nighttime activity but my longings, my agonies, it all gets penned. Mostly I'm just trying to make sense of my existence. Specifically, what parts of my thought processes are Masonic "programming", what parts are demonic, and what parts are just me? At this point I'm wondering if there is a *me* at all.

When the pastor and his wife started visiting me, he'd declare with confidence, "a good friend can do everything a therapist can do." I found that a very odd thing to say, kind of an indictment thrown back onto its owner. The implication seemed to be that I don't have any good friends. But my situation isn't exactly a topic for the coffee klatch. Picturing prim and proper ladies seated around a table at an upscale cafe, I see myself. I walk in and dump a bucket of black ooze on their sunny gathering. "What did you ladies do last night? Me? I had sex with Satan." They'd all look at me in horror. Maybe I don't give my friends enough credit. But just as I reject Steve's repeated suggestion to see a psychologist, I eschew any exposure to my inner world that doesn't involve Brock at its center. There is something very dear and precious about my situation. Like a delicate, wounded child, it requires more than just someone's casual ear and pat answer. I must guard this sacred child with my life. I don't think she can bear any more wounds.

I don't have enough mental energy to care about my friends and their lives. I resent their intrusion in my life. I want to be alone. I want to be with Brock.

***

The driveway loop continues to give me a method for releasing my excess adrenaline. In tears, I propel my body forward and cry out to God, "Why do I have to feel this gargantuan pain? What is the point of it all?"

Then, lying in bed or sitting on the sofa or outside on a lawn chair, I spew words onto the page. *Brock told me I'm "not ready" for healing. How dare he? Bastard.*

Like a thirsty sponge, my trusty journal absorbs my verbose narrative without flinching or judging. Surreptitiously, it feeds me tiny bits of life and nourishment—and a will to survive, to improve and thrive for the sake of my children, out there on the other side of my misery, waiting for their mommy to reemerge.

I think back to when I was a disgruntled teenager decades ago. Although my problems are much larger now, at all times, my accommodating journal has been the recipient of the words that are impossible to say.

***

"You're not ready for healing, Grace, you stupid bitch." I tell myself out loud after a half hour spent going around the loop.

I sit on the rocky ground, grab a pointy rock and slide it across my leg, releasing the tainted blood that circuits my system. It's a self-imposed, self-treatment for my vile existence. After all, only a wicked person would hold on to a posse of appalling demons. All those lies I told myself about being a chaste woman of God are a joke.

Usually it's just deep scratches, but sometimes I'll use a razor blade. The blood that pools on my skin is then used in lieu of a pen to write scathing words to Brock for ignoring me. When Brock sees them, he'll be angry. "These letters are total nonsense," he'll rant. Then when I cry and sound contrite, he'll cool his tone and say something like, "Grace, you've got to promise me that you'll stop cutting."

My promises mean nothing.

***

Despite my best efforts to employ coping skills, the need to flee has become palpable. Before I really know what I'm doing, I'm in the car headed down the driveway, abandoning my children. It tears at me to see the looks on their faces as I go but my sense of love and responsibility have been snuffed out by desperation and agony. Brock has been putting me off for months and I can't take it any longer. I'm headed toward his house, but I don't know if that's where I'll end up. A motel room, a fifth of whiskey, and a razor blade are an equally tempting destination.

The room is minimal but doable. The amber-colored whisky looks almost invisible resting on the similarly-colored bedspread—last decade's color scheme. I pull open the drapes to let the light in, then turn back to the bottle. My mind pictures the cleaning lady coming in in the morning and discovering my lifeless, bled-out body. I play this scenario over and over until it's almost as if the deed is already done. I don't care. The golden liquid will dull the pain of the razor. Dull my inhibitions. Make the job easier.

The telephone sits by the bed, business-like. My eyes veer from the whiskey back to the phone as a surge of possibility vies to commandeer my escape-by-death strategy. I will try, just once. If he's not home, I'm opening the bottle.

"Hello." Brock sounds as if he's expecting my call.

I'm silent. Thinking, judging his tone to see if he's safe.

"Grace, is that you? Where are you? Steve's worried." His voice is tender and invites me to speak.

"I'm in Woodburn. I don't want to die but I don't see any other way. I can't live with this agony any longer. I've just got so much *pain*."

"Why don't you drive down here," Brock says.

Even though that is what I want to hear, the satisfaction is elusive and vague, the possibility is still too foggy.

"I'd like to help you if I can." Brock tries to blow the fog away.

"Okay," I whisper, immediately loathing my neediness once again.

***

The anxiety-triggering landmark is situated as it always is, on that last curve. I'm tempted to just ignore Brock's lane and drive on into the hills in the distance. The news report plays in my head: Wife, mother of four, missing, presumed dead." Steve would remarry and have the wife he deserves. The kids would be better off without me.

Brock opens the door as I approach the steps. He smiles and allows me in.

The living room is tidy as usual and bright with daylight. The picture window frames an abundance of tiny plants emerging in pristine, curvy rows out of a brown carpet that stretches as far as the eye can see. While Marge is engaged with paperwork, Brock talks to me and I feel a sense of ease at being swaddled once again in his fearless world, away from the impending doom back home.

"I want to know about your earthquake panic," Brock states with a detective's gleam in his eye. "I think you might have been tortured with some kind of government sensory-deprivation chamber."

The farther Brock's reality stretches, the happier I am.

Brock has posed several odd theories lately, all stemming from what the Bible says about the End Times. He believes the New World Order is imminent and that when the "call back" occurs, my Masonic, Monarch programming will turn me into a robotic servant, primed to perform the task I've been pre-assigned. How my anxiety over earthquakes fits into this theory, I'm not sure, but Brock has a gift for manipulating the impossible square into a very round hole.

"I think it was cold," I reveal, oblivious as to where that idea comes from. And suddenly I'm shivering. My eyes are closed and I'm locked in some kind of freezer in a laboratory. I'm shaking uncontrollably. I know I'm lying on the carpet in Brock's living room, but I'm also locked away in a cold, dark place. How long I'm like this, I don't know, but when the phone rings, Marge is telling Brock there's an emergency. Brock is out the door, just like that.

Lying on the bed in the guest room, I feel as though the surgeon abandoned me on the operating table. My wound is gaping open, exposed and painful.

Beyond the silence, I keep hearing the incessant roar of a hot rod car, the engine revving over and over again. How long has it been going on before I've even noticed it? More importantly, how do I make it stop?

"I'm going to go home," I tell Brock when he returns late that night. "There's no point in staying here. You've got those other women who need you more than I do."

"Don't leave," Brock demands emphatically, "or I'll have Steve come and get you."

Nothing makes any sense. I'm an adult woman, a wife and mother, but also a needy, sad child. I can't turn my brain off. Raw nerves, Lucifer's faceless people, my children, my dresses, Brock's home, the freezer—the engine just continues revving.

The next day, promptly after Brock sets out to attend to some errand, I say goodbye to Marge and leave. I walk across the highway and make my way down a narrow road that bisects the many farmers' fields situated in this area. About a mile along, a shallow creek intersects the road and I veer off, traipsing through tall grass along the creek's edge. I can hear a car in the distance, so I look for the best place to hide. I crouch down and wait.

I peer at the nearby bushes for the orchid but it's not here. That was Hawaii, years ago, I remind myself. I'm not waiting for the mother and Boyd to leave. I'm a grown woman acting like a teenager. I don't want to be found. I want to flee.

As Brock's footsteps come closer, I give in to my own demise. He walks me back to his house, having assured the policeman that he's got things under control.

True to his word, he sends me packing. Despite my protests and my tears, I am banished.

At home, my emotions surge once more. Not only has Brock abandoned me again, I've got a role to play in the "call back" to usher in the New World Order. There is no hope at all. My future is doomed. There is no hope. Now I *know* I have to end it.

While the babysitter watches my kids, I lumber up to the garage attic, where the box of family photos is situated, the place where I received that much-desired *sign* I was praying for. I concede to my dead, Masonic grandfather. I knew it was futile to try to escape. My destiny was set in stone years ago. Who am I to think I can change my fate?

Cowering in a dark corner, I reach into my pocket for my bottle of sedatives. I twist the lid off and pour them into my mouth. Swallowing the dry, bitter medicine is easier than I thought it would be. I drop the bottle and reach for my razor blade. A line of blood oozes from my wrist. I go deeper and deeper but it never does more than ooze. Hours or minutes, I'm not sure how long before I hear footsteps coming up the stairs. The blood on my arm has jelled. My mind is numb.

A familiar voice interrupts the droning in my head. "Here she is," he yells to the voices downstairs. It's the pastor. He's come to rescue me … but I don't want to be rescued anymore.

***

The ambulance ride to town is strangely calm. The attendee is talking to me casually, as if I've twisted my ankle.

"Can you show me your pill bottle?' she says slightly louder than she needs to.

"Where are we going?" I ask through the fog.

"We're going to the hospital," she says. I detect garlic on her breath.

***

In the Emergency Room, someone sticks a tube down my throat which triggers my impulse to vomit. All the pills and stomach juices come up through the tube and into some kind of receptacle. Then a doctor comes in and lifts my shirt and pushes on my stomach. I want to tell him to get his freaking hands off me but I stay quiet.

"Why do you want to kill yourself?" he asks placidly as if we're discussing some mundane subject like the weather. He must see this kind of thing all the time, I tell myself.

My silence compels him to say, "Not doing so well, are you?"

"No," I whisper and look away.

A little while later, Steve walks in carrying a bag of my belongings. It seems weird seeing him here. He's like a stranger. "The doctor wants you to be admitted to the psychiatric facility."

"Okay." It must be the residual effect of the drugs that leaves me feeling so docile and cooperative.

***

"So tell me what's going on," the handsome young therapist named Ryan says from the chair across from mine. "Your husband Steve says you were having some issues with somebody named Brock. Is that right?"

"Yes. But it's okay now. I'll call him tomorrow."

"Is he helping you?"

"Yeah, he is," I say, scanning the small office. It's tidy and warm. *Congratulations, Grace. Finally, after all these years, you're receiving undivided attention with a* real *therapist. And if anybody needs therapy, God knows it's you.*

"So what things are you and Brock working on?" Ryan asks, scribbling notes on a clipboard.

"He's the only one that understands me. He knows the things I've been through and what my family was like and how—" I abruptly stop. The feeling that I'm making all of this up is overwhelming. The only way to do battle with it is to take on an air of superiority. There is no way in hell I'm going to tell him or anyone else in this place what's really going on. These people are all a bunch of phonies, probably working for the Illuminati or something. They'll just try to take me away from Brock, program me to see him as the enemy. But I doubt Ryan is part of the organization. He's much too nice to be diabolical.

"Is Steve supportive?"

I know what he's fishing for. He wants to know if Steve is abusive.

"Yeah, he's fine," I say almost too cavalierly.

"How about Brock? Has he ever hit you?"

I can feel my face go from baseline to burning in a matter of seconds. I look down to deflect from my skin's obvious color change.

"Why do you ask?" More deflection. I know the answer.

"Just wondering. We therapists like to know these things," he says, smiling.

"Well, yeah, there's been a few times, but he was trying to …," I swallow and breathe. "You know, I can get kind of annoying sometimes and ...," I say, smiling. I breathe again and contemplate how much to tell Ryan. Can I trust him? I sigh, breathe in once more, and continue. "I've got demons. Brock is trying to help me get rid of them. Sometimes it gets physical."

"Like how physical?"

"Well, one time—" I can't. I'm betraying Brock. "It's no big deal. He's not an abuser, if that's what you're wondering."

"Okay," he says.

After some dialog regarding medications, which I staunchly resist, Ryan walks me back to the nurse's station.

"A nurse will show you around in a minute if you want to wait here. Good luck to you, Grace."

"Thanks, Ryan," I say and smile, feeling awkward. I'm officially a nut case.

Across from the nurse's hub is a huge whiteboard with patient names and schedules written with various ink colors. I don't see my name anywhere.

Next to it are two solid doors with the word "Shower" written above them. I wonder if they'll let me use my razor.

I follow the nurse down and around the hallways. I'm lost and disoriented. She assures me that before long I'll know my way around.

The TV is blaring in the lounge area where a few elderly women sit together, smoking and coughing. One is silent, looking down. The other two are looking at the TV. As the days wear on, I take more and more notice of these sad, worn-out members of humanity, wondering why they're here. Have they always been mental patients or are they just getting too old to be alone anymore?

***

Seated across from Roberta, I'm pretty convinced that she's a witch. She's wearing all black. Even her long hair looks like midnight. She wants me to open up and trust her. Yeah, right. What I want is for Ryan to come back. Unfortunately, he was just the intake resident.

"I don't open up to just *anybody*," I state emphatically, aware that I've probably offended her. "I have a hard time trusting people."

"Well, you're safe here."

"Uh-huh. right. I don't even know you. Why would I want to open up and share my secrets with a total stranger? Why don't you tell me something about *you*?" I quip.

"Because this is about *you*."

"Well, what I want is for you to tell me about yourself."

"What do you want to know?" She gives in, shifting in her chair. Even though it wasn't my intention, I've made her uncomfortable and I chuckle to myself because it's kind of cool to have this much power over a witch.

"Well, tell me *something*. Um ... okay. How do you feel about flowers? What's your favorite flower?" I ask, completely serious.

"I don't know. I guess I like geraniums. I've got a pot of red ones at home."

I smile. "See, that wasn't so hard. Now I know a little something about you." What I want to know is if she's a witch, but I'm too scared to ask.

***

Most of my five days in the psych ward are spent pretending to be normal. I talk with the elderly ladies and stay silent during the group sessions. The craft time is stupid but I comply. Somehow, by the time I leave, I've collected a three-inch tall stack of photocopied handouts on various "coping skills." Among them, a signed "contract" stating I will call someone instead of trying to kill myself. I know whom I'll call and I hope he'll be in a good mood. Certainly these last few weeks should have taught him not to fuck with me anymore.

***

Another busy night. The flashbacks were fast and furious but most of them disappeared before I could get them written down. As I check my notepad, the writing is almost illegible.

Guillotine. Yes, I remember this. It felt *very* real, as if I were living it in the present tense.

The rest of the writings are unfamiliar now.

Terror. Hawaii. Night. Bedroom.

Game. I'm it. Something sharp into my hand.

A knife, in mid-air. Something black dangling, a robe's sleeve.

Bedroom. Hollis Street. Something white like a hat with points, a crown? Glowing white.

As hard as I try, I can't remember any of what's written on my notepad. It's like someone else wrote it. I don't understand why these flashbacks—or whatever they are—keep happening. Sometimes I wonder if it's my mind's way of healing itself from my traumatic past. Whether this includes the Masonic events that Brock posits or not, I know there was trauma.

I toss my notepad back on the nightstand and hoist my body out of bed. I will attempt to drown my internal maelstrom by tending to my poor children. I've neglected them and they really deserve better from me.

As I drive the older two to school, Brock sits above my left shoulder, watching. He sees what I see, the oncoming traffic slamming into my car, head-on, full force, my bloody body lying on the pavement, my cheek smashed into the rough, scorching blacktop. It feels very real and I search my mind to see if it really happened and I've just forgotten it. Maybe it happened in my *amnesic* past. A horrific crash, and just this tiny bit of the aftermath is breaking through the arcane barricade in my brain—a flashback by day, perhaps?

A demon of destruction or murder, Brock would likely say.

***

Following my psych ward stint, I resumed my obsession with Brock. Interpreting his mercurial nature, I live my life accordingly. Riding the coattails of a forty-five minute call, I'll either be writing him a letter praising him for his infinite kindness or a scathing rant written with my blood.

When he's in a good mood, he assures me that he's not giving up and that we *will* get to the bottom of it. I just need to trust him and focus on Jesus.

Lately he's been even more talkative, expressing the various subplots of his life. A combination of indebtedness and a looming detachment from my own world render me a great listener. Besides, it's such an honor to have him tell me personal things about himself. I think about how lucky I am compared to all those people vying for his attention. Brock is spending time with *me*. How cool is that?

"People don't understand me," he confesses one day during a particularly animated rant. "I put hundreds of hours into helping you people and all I get is criticism."

Even Marge doesn't understand him sometimes, he tells me. I feel his burden. It mixes with my own as I further lose my grip on reality.

"She doesn't like how much money I spend on calling *you*," he tells me and my compassion explodes in a cloud of guilt and resentment.

But I can't stay angry with Brock. He's helping me. He's God's appointed servant. The photo of my grandfather confirms it.

Sometimes as I run the loop I wonder why Brock bothers with me at all. I mean, what's in it for him? Endless phone calls, bills up the ying-yang, a needy woman constantly clamoring for his time. Hardly a dream job. And Brock certainly isn't getting rich off this ministry, either. He never charges a fee for his deliverance sessions. He feels called by God to give his time freely. I feel very lucky to know him. And perhaps he feels lucky to know Steve and me. After all, a leader needs followers.

CHAPTER TWENTY-THREE

As promised, Brock hasn't given up, for which I'm grateful. I treasure the feeling of being rescued and cared about by a father figure. But I don't tell him this because he doesn't want me to think of him as a father anymore.

He continues his detective duties so he can figure out why the demons refuse to leave, convinced that there is a secret bond that keeps them entrenched. He works with other women that he's sure have also been abused by the Masons. The Masonic demons know all about the Illuminati and the New World Order and Brock tries all kinds of ways to get them to spill.

"These secret societies are comprised of a bunch of legalists," he declares. "They do everything by the book. What happened to one of you happened to all of you. They perform the same ceremonies and install the same demons into all their people."

He briefs me on memory details that the other two women have revealed which in turn triggers my memory—or the demon's memory. Or my own graphic imagination through the power of suggestion.

"Demons always lie," Brock says. So he has to take those details and interpret them into truth. He asks leading questions like "Was there a human sacrifice? Was Josef Mengele presiding?"

I provide answers and once he's convinced that he knows the most relevant of facts, including the demon's name, he commands it to admit defeat.

Many of the demons have biblical names. Brock claims these secret societies are counterfeiting the Bible's end time prophesies. *Eloheim* or *I Am* or *Legion*, these are some of the names that have come up. There's always something new to learn from these demons, some kind of newly-discovered key Brock uses to dismantle the diabolical hierarchy in me and the other women. Each revelation is more bizarre than the last.

"I think you're going to have to tie me down so you can fight this demon," I tell Brock one night.

"What? You mean, tie you to a chair or something?"

"Yep. That's exactly what I mean." I want to illustrate to Brock that I'm willing to do anything to get free, including being roped to a chair and humiliated the entire night under a bright light with a group of people worshiping God.

"Did it leave?" he'll ask as he always does, while I see daylight forming on the horizon through the slight gap in the drapes.

There are times when it feels like something is happening. I feel a faint sense of release. Other times I'll see something in my mind's eye, an amorphous form slipping into the depths.

But the demons never really leave. The symptoms might improve for a few hours but things always revert to how they've always been.

***

"You are Josef Mengele's daughter," Brock declares one night as we sit in his living room. Based on a book he's reading and one of the other women's most recently recovered memories, he believes that Mengele's is the highest of the Illuminati bloodlines. "This is all about creating a master-race," he tells me. "When you truly believe you're part of the bloodline and that Josef Mengele is your father, you'll be ready for a healing service. Right now I want you to go home and think about it and get yourself prepared."

As I turn onto the highway headed for home, I have lots of time to ponder Brock's latest conjectures. I can't help toying with an inkling of pride with the notion of being part of the master race. Being superior, having above-average blood coursing through my veins, although admittedly a foreign concept, feels kind of good.

But then I have to laugh. Me? I hardly think so. "Wouldn't a person with above-average blood also be equipped with above-average intelligence? This would *so not* describe me," I say out loud to the Brock above my shoulder watching me speed down the highway. "Plus, she'd have to be gorgeous, like Charlize Theron in *The Devil's Advocate*. I look more like that middle-aged colleague of Keanu Reeves' character.

Actually, I look more like the father's side of the family. I'd be more inclined to believe I have a different *mother* than a different father.

I sigh and keep my eyes focused on the road.

Like trying to drop a 747 jet on our rural property and make it look as if it's always been there, Brock's theories leave me pining for logic to make them fit with my existence as I know it. It's grueling always trying to figure out who I am, trying to squeeze my history into Brock's cleverly crafted mold.

Worse than that is what it does to my psyche. I'm too far down the food chain to confidently know who I am or where I came from. My most basic, primal beliefs are suspect. I'm incapable of forming my own reality. This is devastating.

Tears are streaming down my face. I'm not sure which devastation they're resulting from, leaving Brock again or my own insanity.

I suppose Josef Mengele *could* be my real father.

Suddenly I'm remembering the mother's brief history lesson. *Stormy night, seven pounds seven ounces, all black and blue.* Did she make that up? Was she always so quick and annoyed because she, like me, hated lying? Was it a lie? Was she "programmed" to rattle off this narrative to appease my childishness? Could the mother's prolonged aloofness be a result of her Masonic connections? Do I remind her of a ritual rape performed by Josef Mengele? No wonder she doesn't want anything to do with me.

As I veer off the freeway onto the adjoining highway heading east, the Kleenex I've been grasping has performed well beyond its capabilities. I toss it aside and grab the hem of my shirt to wipe my eyes and the snot off my nose. I blink several times to keep the tears from obstructing my view of the road.

I miss Brock already. I want to be close to him. The further I drive, the more agonized I feel.

I hardly ever think about the father. He's always been enveloped in his own world, his own comings and goings. We're amicable at Christmas, cordial, not much more than that. That is all he is, a friendly acquaintance.

I think of the hazy black and white photo of Mengele that Brock showed me. Is this the man I saw when I had that very first night terror while babysitting so many years ago? The dark-haired man in a white lab coat, right outside the trailer? Is Mengele the man I was so frightened of?

***

While I'm folding clothes, my youngest, now a lively toddler, wraps herself around my leg. I stop, sigh and pick her up. She's adorable, her red hair a testament to her true inheritance, her father's daughter. I squeeze her and think of the gift she's been given: a daddy who loves her. She'll never be plagued with the emotional baggage I carry, thank God.

I straighten her downy locks and carry her to the sofa. After using the scissors to trim her hair, she's been lovingly dubbed "Miss No-Bangs." I grab a book off the floor and read her a story.

If there's one thing I've learned, it's how vulnerable and impressionable children are. I was much too harsh with my older two when they were toddlers. It pains me how they suffered because of my stupidity. I can't go back and redo those years but I can do better now.

I know I have to get away from Brock. I've stopped calling him so often, instead investing my energies in running the loop or tending to my kids, going shopping or working in the garden—anything to keep me from feeling horrific abandonment.

Running the driveway loop, I'm proud of the telltale path my feet have carved. I appreciate its familiarity, how it provides a sense of place in my weird world, even if this place is so far from Brock. The bare earth, devoid of gravel, reminds me of the roads Adam and I forged for our Lilliputian worlds decades ago. I suppose in both instances, they're an attempt at avoiding the complications of life by creating a tolerable, tangible one.

***

It's been a few weeks since Brock declared my Illuminati bloodline heritage. Bizarre images and sensations are invading my consciousness, such as carvings on my bones. "A sort of branding," Brock says. I'm remembering lab experiments involving needles in the eyes and extracting fertile eggs from young girls' ovaries. I'm not sure if I'm the victim or the perpetrator of these events, or maybe both. They feel real and fabricated simultaneously. If it weren't for my kids and my need to retain some semblance of consistency for them, I'm sure I'd be declared a paranoid lunatic. Somehow my desire to be a functional mother keeps just enough of my head above the pool of insanity to avoid that.

At the library, I grab a few books on World War II, hoping they'll reveal something about "my father." I'd like to know what he looked like in the 1960s, when I would have seen him. It sickens me, reading about the atrocities he and fellow SS Nazis inflicted on an innocent race of people. Yet I'm drawn to him in a perverse way. I suppose that proves that I'm demon possessed or that his blood is indeed flowing through my veins. When it becomes overwhelming, I have to get away, outside to purge myself of this tainted blood. I don't want to be a member of an evil bloodline.

Over the phone, Brock reminds me how I promised him I wouldn't cut myself anymore.

"I want you to stop that cutting," he says, annoyed. "You're off focus. You need to listen to me."

Like a tornado that leaves an eerie calm in its wake, Brock's voice grows softer and attends to my wreckage. He compassionately retells Bible stories of being grafted into God's family, iterating that no evil is too much for Jesus' sacrifice on the cross, that any and all can come before the foot of the cross. He implores me to *believe* so the demon will lose power. He wants to rescue me, see me free.

"When you're ready, we'll have a healing service," he assures me.

"I'm ready" I tell him. I want to say that I've been ready for five fucking years, but I know better than to rip apart this tender moment with my sarcasm.

What Brock really means is that I'll be ready when *he* declares that I am. At some point, he'll note a humbled contriteness in my attitude and that will be the sign that I'm truly ready to receive God's deliverance.

When I'm ready, I replay over in my mind. God, I hate that son of a bitch. How the hell is he going to know if I'm ready if he never even talks to me?

Once again, I'm circling the loop, angry. *How dare he? Asshole. I hate his guts. He thinks he knows me so well but the truth is, it's all about him. He's got those other women who are much more … whatever. I'm just an irritant. A pesky mosquito that keeps buzzing around his head, a pest he'd like to annihilate.*

Damn it. I should have stretched my legs a little first. I can feel them cramping up. I drop down to a fast walk, shaking them alternately as I go. Looking down at my well-worn path, I angrily kick at the ground and mess it up. I hate my life.

Usually I'm aware of how long I'm out here but because it's a Saturday and Steve is home to watch the kids, I'm free to rant as long as I need to.

Why did you bring Brock into my life anyway, God? To torture me? I thought you were supposed to be a loving God, I mentally scream at the clouds, stumbling over an occasional rock.

He's meeting with one of the other women, I bet.

A slight breeze cools my burning body. The motion of the clouds makes the sunlight come and go as I continue to propel myself forward.

I'm crying, thinking about a recent call when, as calmly as possible, I asked Brock if we could schedule appointments. "So when the abandonment feelings get intense," I told him, "I can focus on and take comfort in knowing we've got a prearranged date for our next session."

"I don't cower to demons," he scowled.

The wound cuts deep into my soul. I keep picturing a giant zipper running the length of my body. No matter how much I will myself to do so, I just can't seem to open it and crawl out.

As I continue walking, it suddenly occurs to me why I've been unable to get free of demonic oppression. The demons aren't *in* me. The demons *are* me. I. Am. A. Demon. No wonder the evil spirits—identified with whatever name Brock appoints to them—won't let go. They're not a separate entity to be cast into the pit of hell, *they're me.* And I'm them. We're one. Of course. It all makes sense now.

Tears stream down my shell as the full impact of this revelation takes hold. I don't exist. There is no me. I am a demon posing as a human, existing in a human body. I am what a demon looks and acts like, feels like—thinks like.

Continuing my fast-paced walk, I let the ugly reality set in. I search my brain for a resting place, a mental juncture where I can go to find goodness and joy, but there is none. No such place exists because it is all swathed in Masonic, Illuminati, Mengele evil. It's who I am. The demons have been fooling me into thinking I'm a human being. Everything good that I've believed about myself, my core beliefs, my anchor in the sea of uncertainty, was just delusion. Demons are good at deluding people. Brock even says so. "They hang on to deceit," he said.

I sit down, take off my shoes and socks, hunt around for the sharpest rock I can find, and begin methodically slicing into my foot. Bleeding out is the only thing that makes sense.

***

Lying in bed, my reality begins to settle into itself. Like a receding flood, the bitter water seeps down below the surface, into the depths.

Losing oneself is a strange thing, and existing as something unseen is a rather exclusive way to live, I suppose. I wonder what kind of governmental projects I'm a part of. Maybe now that I'm aware of my position as a demon, I'll also be aware of what's going on in this other life I've been living.

I roll over and breathe, allowing the concept of my mystical existence to form itself into reality. I've got to believe that Mengele is my father if I want to get free. I'm dizzy.

Again I'm reminded of my science teacher's peculiar missive decades ago. "Maybe we were created yesterday with a memory to go with it."

CHAPTER TWENTY-FOUR

"Maybe God has other plans for me," I suggest to Brock over the phone while the trees beyond the window bear the brunt of a merciless wind. My daughters are frightened, no doubt because they've witnessed their mother's anxiety disorder at full throttle. I try to comfort them while engaged with Brock. It's been a while since we've spoken. As he is my lifeline, I can't risk cutting our conversation short, even if it is to attend to my kids' needs.

"I mean, maybe there's something I'm supposed to learn from this. There has to be some reason I'm not healed yet."

"We haven't gotten to the bottom of it," he says, abdicating me from the fault he so easily douses me with at other times.

"Well, I want you to know," I state emphatically, "that several days ago I realized that I'm not plagued by demons, *I am a demon*."

"Hogwash," Brock swiftly replies in his low, gravelly tone.

I feel a rush of emotions ranging from gratitude to murderous rage. Why is he always so quick to disagree with me? Doesn't he realize that just reinforces my belief that I am a demon?

"This is why I can't trust you and why I'm always sabotaging things," I lament, in tears.

"You're thinking too much. You need to just trust me."

"Okay," I say. "But I don't trust you. I never have."

"Well, you need to just make up your mind to. Have I abandoned you yet?"

"No."

"Then stop believing the lies and trust me. I want you to calm down and stay focused. If you want to get healed, you've got to believe on faith. Does God want to heal you?"

"I think so," I mumble, then immediately regret my answer. Brock wants a definitive warrior-type answer, not a feeble *I think so*. I'm just too exhausted to care.

***

Steve knocks on Brock's door to announce us. I hang back, plagued by a combination of shame, anxiety, and anger. I'm completely aware of Brock's experimental ceremonies and the submission they require. It will be another night of humiliation, at best, while the fine art of healing continues to elude me. But one thing's for sure, if I don't at least try, I could miss my healing. I'll hold on to the hope that tonight is *the* night.

Brock has finally deemed me ready, which is a miracle in itself, especially given the fact that I'm dealing with a boatload of pent-up anger.

As I stand on the periphery, Brock explains the night's agenda to what appears to be an interested crowd. He seems satisfied with his followers and their rapt attention.

I offer a brief smile to one of the women. I hold in check the cynical remark on the tip of my tongue because other than Brock's voice, it's dead silent in here.

"The goal of tonight's ceremony is to reenact a near-death experience," Brock says with confidence. "The way it will work is three men and myself will hold each woman under the water until we feel them starting to fight for air. At that point we'll keep them down just long enough that they feel like they're dying. In the dark, with a full moon overhead, this will reverse the ritual that occurred when they were kids and should force the demons to leave."

His logic is flawed at best, but I lack the ability to decipher it. Besides, I can't trust what goes on in my head. Who am I to tell Brock what to do? I'm a demon

As people head out to their cars for the short drive to the creek, I walk over to Brock and ask him if he'll ride with Steve and me because I haven't seen him in a while.

"I'm riding with Gena," he tells me, then looks at Steve. "She's worried that someone is going to kill her."

This fuels my demonic anger. but I don't say anything.

The August air is still warm even with the onset of nightfall. The moon hovers like a beacon above us. As we walk to the creek, one of the other women notes the government helicopters flying overhead. In defiance, I wave to them while she shivers in fear.

At the creek, I can see Brock and a few other men several feet out. As I slog through the waist-high water toward them, I can't help but feel like the whole thing is stupid. I'm mad that Brock won't pay any attention to me and that Gena, the drama queen, is always his highest priority.

Moonlight shimmers on the surface of the water and the smell of algae takes me back to my childhood and the father's terrifying swimming lessons. But I'm not a child any longer. The feelings of anger and rebellion sabotage the required contriteness of this sacred event.

Brock is saying something, praying maybe; I'm not sure. I'm hovering above myself, deafened by my own insubordination as I ruminate on how pissed off I am.

Without warning, the communion bread still in my mouth, a bevy of hands plunges my body into the icy water. Instantly, I'm the little girl again, learning to swim, baffled by my father's actions. Fueled entirely by involuntary reflexes, I flail and fight, my panic causing a torrent of splashes and bubbles, magnified a hundredfold under the water. And then the adult me finally realizes that I was totally unprepared for the distress Brock's latest procedure is intended to cause.

"I need to catch my breath," I yell to Brock and the other men assigned to hold me under. They keep trying to grab me and shove my head back under the water.

"Wait! I need to catch my breath!" I repeat at the top of my burning lungs, completely aware that being agitated and not able to breathe is the whole point of the exercise.

Finally, either my panic wins or the men figure I'm hopeless. They let go and I fill my lungs with night air. Water drips off my nose and I rub my eyes as I trudge my leaden body toward the shore. Keeping my gaze away from onlookers, I search for a way to flee this insanity.

With only a few more steps to dry land, I stop. I can't miss my healing. I turn and wade back to Brock and the other men. I'm prepared now, I tell myself. I'll do it right this time.

"Just let me … catch my ... breath," I beg.

But the second time is no different than the first. I fail once again.

Back in the car, I cower in the backseat, completely undone, humiliated. I'm sure Gena performed flawlessly, of course. I just don't have what it takes. God is disappointed with me. I lack the faith I need to get healed. I'm too rebellious. Brock has told me so many times. Now he's got proof.

***

As Steve and I drive home, I try to make sense of my fucked up life. I'm addicted to Brock in the worst way but I'm also a free spirit. And the two don't mix. I'm baffled by my flawless ability to sabotage myself and I'm helpless over this crazy, forbidden draw to Brock. Maybe it's part of the demonic possession, or a curse or something. Perhaps I was "programmed" to need a handler and Brock unwittingly stepped into that role when he originally agreed to see me.

The fact that the whole situation is so taboo, so socially unrecognized and unacceptable just plays in to my feelings of despair. Unlike sex abuse, religious abuse is not against the law. Up until tonight, I've been uncertain if indeed Brock's methods are abusive. But I think there's something seriously wrong with using water-trauma as a method of healing.

I remember how I asked God for a confirmation that working with Brock was his will. I was sure that the photo of my grandfather was it. Maybe I was wrong.

I'm hopelessly addicted to Brock but I don't even know where to go for help. The person I'm asking to help me get well is the person who's making me sicker. It's dizzying.

How much easier my life would be if I were fighting an addiction to an inanimate object such as drugs or alcohol, or even a behavioral addiction such as gambling, shopping, or sex. Professionals have erected treatment facilities and support groups for these types of compulsive behaviors. I've got a cult-minded addiction to another person. If a facility exists for people addiction, I've sure never heard of it.

***

"You're no worse off," Brock tells me over the phone the next day.

"You weren't under water that long," I hear Marge say in the background. Of course she's going to absolve her husband of any wrong-doing. At this moment, I want to bash her face in.

I want Brock's attention. I crave it. But it always ends up hurting me.

In response to my dismal efforts to find clarity, Brock always says, "You think too much." But how can I *not*? I'm trying to sort out my reality, my identity, my truth.

Is anything I remember about my history real?

The reality I'm supposed to embrace without question is living inside Brock's head, not mine. Is it any wonder I'm so inordinately dependent upon him to feed me bits of it on a regular basis? Over-dependence, addiction. I can't survive without him. I can't *think* without him. I don't exist without him.

CHAPTER TWENTY-FIVE

It's the end of a decade, the end of a century, and nearing the end of an era. Hazel, one of the women needing Brock's help, is seated beside me in the backseat of Brock's car. We're on the way to the airport so she can catch her flight home.

Although my healing remains elusive, I've been trying to combat my selfishness by supporting the other women Brock is helping. Recently, Brock has spent many hours attending to Hazel's need for deliverance.

On the sidelines, I could feel myself cringe at Brock's curtness as he raked poor Hazel over the coals.

Does he treat me this way, too? Of course he does, I hear myself say.

Brock is quiet, concentrating on driving. I don't want Hazel to go home without some kind of freedom. She's plagued with recurring migraines and fibromyalgia. Can't he say something to ease her distress before she has to leave? Her time is almost up.

"Hazel has another migraine this morning, Brock," I say.

"You irritate me," is Brock's quick retort.

I can hear Hazel utter a quiet moan, the sentiment of someone who knows how biting Brock's remarks can be.

He launches into a diatribe about programming or whatever. I'm not really listening. I'm picturing an old fashioned aluminum garbage can so crammed with trash that, no matter how hard I try, the lid simply will not seal what's inside. Additional bits of garbage litters the ground next to it, stuff that has fallen out during my unsuccessful struggle to secure the cover.

I speak quietly to Hazel and Marge occasionally, but I can't even look at Brock. I keep picturing the garbage can, overflowing with refuse.

With that final pejorative, something inside me crumbles. Call it my will, my determination, my stubbornness, my heart. The garbage can that corrals seven years of insults and contradictions and confusions has finally reached its limit.

The rejection is agonizing but it's reached a point of anger and clarity, too. There is no pleasing Brock. As long as I'm under his influence, I'll always be his victim, the fatherless daughter scratching for attention. Sadly, this is the only role I know how to play.

When Brock, Marge, and I arrive back at their house, I offer a quick goodbye and go to my car. Marge seems a bit dismayed. Brock heads straight for the front door and says nothing.

Unlike my customary departure routine which includes horrendous sadness and gazing longingly through the rear view mirror, this time I keep my gaze straight ahead. It's over.

***

I spend a lot of time thinking about my identity, who I am, who I was and who I want to be. I'm also rethinking my faith.

Like a toddler attempting its first steps I'm hesitant, wobbly, worried that my gait might lead me straight into another blindsided screw-up. I can see that I possess a penchant for sabotaging my life and my relationships. I suppose it's my fringe thinking still looking for a reason to exist and a place to belong. But now I'm beginning to think it's okay if I don't belong anywhere.

Although the proximity between Brock and me has widened, his message lingers, attempting to usurp my resolve. "I need him. I *still* need him. I don't trust anyone. I can't trust myself. I don't know who or what the enemy is."

Everyone is the enemy. That's what people believe when they're in a cult. And it's what they still believe when they leave it.

CHAPTER TWENTY-SIX

It's going to be a nice day. Soaking up the fresh morning air, I feel glad to be alive. Standing on my backyard deck, I sip my coffee and survey my surroundings. In the fore, my modest garden sprawl bursts with admittedly too many plants in too little space. Funny, I can't seem to get things exactly right. I'm beginning to believe that the pursuit of gardening—altering Nature's conventions—is a huge lesson in futility. The fact that I enjoy it so much, even with its challenges and persistent absurdities, must say something about my stubbornness. I chuckle, take another deep breath and another sip of coffee while making a mental list of jobs to tackle.

I raise my eyes and look into the distance. Beyond the neighbor's house, down the hill, past the tree tops, across the river, the valley's landscape stretches and yawns until it disappears into foothills and fog. Somewhere in that general direction is Brock's home.

My sunny day just went dark.

I need to just forget everything, I tell myself. There's no point in rehashing all of the pain and shame and misunderstandings that occurred while I was working with Brock. I need to just let go and move on. But deep within, I have an insistent longing for this man who turned my world upside down. It's a residual shadowy yearning that tears me up. Reminding myself of the years of bullshit I went through doesn't relieve this inescapable need to be with him. If anything, it makes it worse. I miss him and Marge. And although I give my pursuit of gardening a valiant effort, it doesn't seem to be the cure for this terrible aching.

There were good times. I smile, remembering the Christmas gathering when Brock took a Pirouette cookie off the tray and pretended to smoke it. We all laughed and I took a picture of him posing like a mob boss. Or the time he ran to the freezer, brought out a carton of ice cream and pointed to it in hopes of getting our team to shout "ice cream" and win the game. What game was it? I can't remember now.

Despite all of the drama with Brock, I felt a strong sense of familiarity and belonging with him and Marge. I wonder if this is what having parents feels like, that sense of knowing that, no matter what, the hub is always there. Stretch your wings far and wide, explore the vast reaches of life's offerings, but home will always welcome your return. Perhaps that is the big draw of cults and gangs, being surrounded by like-minded people with the comfort and stability and purpose that it affords. I'm pretty sure that having a sense of calm belonging is an archetypal need.

The club that demanded I sacrifice myself to its leader should have raised some flags, but I was too absorbed in watering my parched psyche to see them.

Too often, I toy with a secret desire for reconciliation. My fantasy involves Brock contacting me without provocation on my part. Of his own volition, he owns up to his wrongdoing and genuinely apologizes, and the walls and egos are shattered, paving the way for mutual respect. Day after day I hope the apology will come, but it doesn't.

Sometimes I contemplate making arrangements that will facilitate things, resuscitate what appears, as time wears on, to be a rotting corpse. I'll phone him and declare how I feel and he'll admit to his wrongdoing.

It's only with fierce willpower and a constant stream of reality checks from Steve that I don't cave in and make that call. It's interesting, but the longer I remain resolute, the more empowered I feel. It's nice to sit in the driver's seat.

My relationship with Brock demanded I play a submissive role. I donned the cloak of compliance the day he and I met, consenting to my own victimization. As a grown woman, I should have known better. At this point, I'm not really sure if I'm capable of any role but a submissive one with Brock. It's that uncertainty that keeps me planted at home. I'm tired of being a victim.

Okay, enough of all that, I tell myself, setting my empty mug on the deck railing, Of course the ruminations over Brock never cease altogether, but at least I'm not bedridden with depression any longer. I can multi-task. I grab my gloves, trowel, and bucket and head down the path. Willow, the garden cat, follows closely behind me.

Sometimes I wonder if humans have an innate need to fix things. We seem to have this festering obligation to sort out life's jumbled puzzle pieces and form them into something whole, comprehensible, even beautiful. I've always had the desire to know things on a deeper level. That was part of the problem with my relationship to Brock. It was difficult, if not impossible, for me to take his word for things. As much as I wanted to trust him carte blanche, I needed to understand the gritty details, the reasons for the diagnoses, the evidence that led to the verdict. I pined for logical answers to the myriad questions running through my mind. I wanted things to make sense. I *still* want things to make sense.

Whenever I'd voice my doubts to Brock, he'd say, "You have more than enough evidence." I suppose he meant that my symptoms and the answers he'd received from the demons were all the proof I needed—or should need.

It was foolish on my part to expect Brock to feel the anguish going on in my head, my ambiguity, shame and confusion. To him everything made perfect sense. But rather than his abrasive, "You over-think everything, Grace," I wish his response would have been, "Really? Tell me about this doubt you feel." Maybe having the safety to discuss it with him would have brought resolution.

With a sudden rise in adrenaline, the tiny weeds emerging from the pathway rocks receive the brunt of my anger. *You over-think everything, Grace,* I replay in my mind with an emphasis on the sarcasm of it. Damn him!

My anger reinforces my resolve. I'm not finished with this. I may be guilty of over-thinking, but too damn bad. It's my life and I'm going to figure out what the hell is going on. I'm going to get to the bottom of my flashbacks and the sleep disorder, the images of violence and cutting, the reasons why I still feel so much anxiety and impending doom. And I want to know for certain whether Brock was correct when he identified me as a victim of ritual abuse and demonic possession. I have no certainty about any of it. I need to know. The ambiguity I feel will only be cured with answers. I'm not sure how to go about obtaining them, but I've got to try.

Suddenly my back is aching. I rise and stretch and feel gratified that the once-thriving weeds have met their demise in my trusty bucket. If only clearing my psyche of its obstacles were so easy.

Willow reemerges from somewhere and nuzzles against my legs. I reach down to pet her, ignoring the strain in my back. She's such a trusted garden friend.

I can see bits of unwanted green around the base of two rose bushes, so I go over to clear them, keeping mindful of the menacing thorns protruding from the stems.

A neighbor starts up his lawnmower, drowning out the birdsong I wasn't really hearing until now, when it's usurped by this maddening machine. I hate lawnmowers with all their noisy, violent cutting and icky exhaust.

It takes a few minutes to calm myself.

The move to this new house was a welcome change, but I wasn't prepared for the culture shock of going from ten acres of seclusion to the suburbs with neighbors in close proximity. I'm grateful that they're quiet, friendly people. The wives have even asked me to join them for their weekly get-togethers over coffee and crafts. If only I could. By refusing their offer, I fear I've offended them, but I still feel incredibly flawed and weird and tainted among the mainstream.

Worse, I feel as though I don't exist outside my anguish. On the rare occasion when I find myself in a social situation, the internal mandate will kick in and I bury my own maelstrom of issues and morph into a veneer of urbanity, going through the social motions to appease this person I've allowed myself to come face to face with. It's an auto-response, a default mechanism, honed by years of practice and maybe a bit of DNA. I recall the mother was also this way, with her painted lips and perma-smile.

There is no me. It takes an enormous amount of effort to portray this normal, socially engaging blob of affability.

Once I'm back in seclusion, the emotions come surging back and I resent having shoved myself aside for the sake of normalcy. I know it's not right to blame the other person, but I do. If only they would stop talking long enough to see the *me* hidden under all of these invisible wounds.

I hate the void, the nothingness. If I'm alone, I feel awful but at least I *feel*. I suppose there is a healthier way to deal with this but, for now, this is the best I can do.

Spending so many hours in the garden probably isn't appropriate, either. I've concluded that nothing I do will feel right and that most likely I'll always have to battle guilt and feelings of inadequacy. Or maybe not always. Maybe at some point I'll gain a measureable amount of confidence that I'm okay. Or I'll get tired and bitter and tell everyone to rot in hell.

Despite the gains I've made post-Brock, I'm still plagued by this paranoid *us versus them* narration playing in my head. I don't know who the *them* are and the fact that they remain so elusive, playing these mind games with me, is unnerving. They don't want to come out. They want to stay under the radar and toy with me from a distance.

When I look for their signs, I find them everywhere. For instance, after many years of abstaining from television, I can watch it now and spot the conspiracy messages with ease. The symbology, the phrases, the codes, they're all blatantly obvious to me. At first they scared me to death, although lately I'm developing just a tiny bit of anger about it all. Perhaps this is how I'll free myself of the paranoia. Maybe anger is the way to empower the victim.

The murders, freak accidents, and missing-persons reports announced almost daily on the news are just cover stories for the ritual killings that occur at some high-up cult meeting somewhere. Never believing anything at face value, I see every news item through the lens of skepticism, knowing the public is being fed a bunch of bullshit by the media.

I wonder which of my neighbors are part of the amorphous *them*. I listen at night, noting which cars arrive home during the wee hours. I watch for telltale behaviors, the signs of involvement. But because I don't really know what those signs are, I assume all my neighbors are *them*.

All older men are abusers, especially church-going older men. They're pedophiles, ritually raping their grandkids all the while playing a role of importance within the church and community. No one would suspect these men, but I know they're evil, every single one of them. Church is full of them.

I can't let my kids out of my sight. It would only take a second for one of the furtive *them* to drive by, grab my precious baby and, poof, they'd be gone. I'd be left to agonize over my child's disappearance and imagine what kind of horrendous torture they'd be forced to endure because I didn't follow through with my cult assignments, whatever those might be.

I pay attention to the images and sounds skipping through my conscious, but relaxed mind, usually while in bed at night. Lately it's a series of random beeps. Steve says I'm describing Morse code. Even while camping, snuggled within the folds of a sleeping bag, I hear those incessant beeps. I wish I could decipher what messages they're sending me.

I'm certain that my feelings of impending doom are coming from the radio waves being broadcast by *them* into the receiver lodged in my head somewhere. All movies are forms of subtle brainwashing. Home computers are still too new to be suspect but if I continue on this paranoid journey, I'm sure I'll find a demon under that doily, too.

For the next five years, I continue my double life. For the sake of my children, I take tentative steps into the mainstream. I so desperately want them to have a normal, healthy childhood. My inadequacies pain me. I discover that as long as I am able to return to the solitude of my garden, I can handle short bouts of social situations. I do it for them.

I see a few counselors, nice enough women, but I can't reveal everything I know because they'd throw me in a padded cell and lose the key.

CHAPTER TWENTY-SEVEN

Self-contempt rises like a bad case of the flu. I swallow, sigh, and inch into an empty parking space. Getting here is the hardest part, I remind myself, breathing deep and shutting off the engine.

For a second, I sit, get my bearings, and gather the dignity to forge ahead. Needing help is so demeaning. I feel like a total failure for not being able to get past this on my own—and not really being sure if getting help is really okay.

Risk requires tenacity. Get out. Walk in the door. *Go*, I chide, impatient with my hesitation.

Everything is spotless, professional, legitimate. *Legitimate.* That is why I'm here. I need legitimate. Yet I'm still antsy because I feel incredibly *illegitimate*. How brazen of me to come here and sully this place.

I've checked in. The receptionists seem nice. Not overly friendly, but not terse, either. A snooty receptionist would make things much more difficult. It's pathetic that I would still allow a person that much power over me, but I'm not very strong right now.

I wait. Music from the '70s emanates softly from hidden speakers. Peter Frampton's "Ooh, baby, I love your way" takes me back to Jayne's domain. I'm seventeen and my journal pages receive my heartbreak. And then, *snap*, I'm middle-aged. I never thought I'd make it this far.

My mind drifts to Brock for a second as I thumb through a magazine. By keeping my distance, my need for him has diminished substantially. I sigh, grateful for the freedom, but also saddened by how foolish I was to trust him.

The doctor's boyish good looks belie his wall of framed achievements and qualifications. His office is tastefully decorated with soft lighting and plump, leather furniture, designed, I'm sure to induce a relaxed, divulging state of mind. I'm glad that I'm not vulnerable to another father figure.

He smiles, asks me how I'm doing. There's no detectable judgment on his face, which I find baffling. I'm not used to this. What I *am* used to are lengthy sermons, lectures about my lack of faith and intolerance to change. The freedom this doctor offers is actually distressing. A bird with an open cage, I'm supposed to fly. I'm supposed to know *how* to fly … but I don't. I hold back, unsure of what lies out there beyond this self-imposed shield. Despite the doctor's non-threatening demeanor, I can picture him quickly rising out of his chair, taking his hand, and slapping it across my face.

There are things I need to work out. I'm really confused, *still*, after five years away from Brock, about how much of his assessment of my life was true. I don't know what, if anything, can I hold on to and what I should dismiss as part of his megalomania.

And if my mixed-up reality weren't enough, I've still got this damn anxiety, this unwelcome resident, perfectly attuned to my vulnerabilities, persistently strumming the panic wire in my brain. I have little mini-flashbacks where feel it happening again, the rumbling or the smell of smoke or any of the host of other triggers. Brock told me I was forced into some kind of sensory deprivation chamber where my panic was monitored and tested. Shortly thereafter, I saw visions of the very thing he suggested. Was it possible that those were just manufactured as a way to explain my anxiety or to please Brock? I don't really own my history. Brock owned it and still owns it.

I'd like it back.

Seated across the room from the doctor, I feel like a shell. I have nothing stored for reference. I need him to tell me what to think and feel, what to believe. But he doesn't tell me and he also doesn't launch in to his latest theories or discuss the other people he's seeing. He doesn't deliver a guilt trip about my lack of faith. He doesn't do any of the things Brock did, which frustrates me. I'm perplexed as to exactly who I am and what I'm doing here.

To remedy the uncomfortable silence, I set words adrift. They float around the room like a cloud of butterflies, airborne and awaiting the swish of a net so they can be seen up close.

I'm sure the doctor doesn't like me. I annoy him with my senseless verbosity. He wishes I'd go away. He's got a stack of papers on his desk behind a burgeoning schefflera and I'm sure he'd like to get to them. If I'd just shut up and get the hell out of his office he could get on with his work. But I keep talking. And he keeps listening.

"I'm sorry for talking so much," I tell him.

"Talking is exactly what you're supposed to do," he tells me.

He has no idea how relieved I am to hear those words.

It takes a while, but, eventually, as I grasp the concept of talk therapy, I see in this man someone who is the antithesis of my history, well trained in—and possibly even gifted with—the fine art of listening. I come to realize how much I need to talk, how beneficial this burgeoning trust is, and how refreshing it is to have a professional on tap to help me sort out the mysteries of my existence.

***

With the doctor's gentle nudging, I unearth my history and lay it all out. But it's all just talk. I don't really feel any of it, except for the sense that I'm betraying myself with my cavalier data-dump. I jabber on as if it's no big deal, even though it's huge. Catastrophic. And yet the tears remain corked and the box of Kleenex sits untouched on the table between us.

"It's all about changing how you think, isn't it?" I posit, remembering the *mindset*, one of Brock's crowning tenets.

"Not entirely. Typically, when you challenge engrained thoughts and behaviors, you're confronted with emotional fallout."

Interesting. Brock constantly urged me to change my beliefs, thoughts, and behaviors. After a short bout of lame obedience, my emotions would surge. I couldn't understand why I was so emotionally volatile. I hated my emotions because they always got in the way of my healing, my compliance, and of being accepted by Brock. And because I hated my emotions, I hated myself. Self-mutilation followed. Eventually I just shut down altogether and decided I must be a demon.

"It would be good if you took some time every day to get in touch with your emotions. Recognize what you're feeling. Don't ignore it. Just feel it."

I know the doctor is giving me good advice because there, cached behind my own urbane defense mechanisms is Emotional Peril. Suppressed, ignored, misunderstood, avoided pain—pulsing, trying to bubble up. I force it down. It's a visceral force and I'm not sure I want to face it. But if I don't, I might become so toxic that no one dares to come near me.

"Expressing your emotions is not a sign of weakness," the doctor tells me. "It takes a lot of courage to confront your feelings. Ideally, it would be good to work through them here in my office."

"Brock didn't really like my emotions, at least my anger. Every time I'd lose it, he'd get pissed off and then I'd get a lecture about how I wasn't being submissive. I think one of the reasons I hide my emotions is because I don't want to be thought of as a whiner—you know, one of those people always moaning about how terrible life is. Besides, my life *isn't* terrible. I've got a great husband and four healthy children, enough money, and a nice home. So why am I so damned depressed?"

"It's more challenging for someone with a *good* life to come to terms with their anxiety and depression than for someone with a difficult life," the doctor declares.

"Makes sense. And why do I have all these racing thoughts of death and torture all the time? I feel guilty. I shouldn't feel this awful when I've got it so good."

"Have you considered medication? The symptoms you're describing sound like they could be biological."

I used to believe drugs were a cop-out for the weak and gullible. Even though I was hearing more and more that anxiety and depression were recognized medical conditions, I didn't want to believe that the remedy was in a pill bottle.

***

"I'm not having that constant anxiety anymore," I tell the doctor a few months after starting on meds. "I'm not so worried about my kids. I can get through a whole day without becoming obsessed with death or catastrophe. I feel like for the first time in my life, my brain is working the way it's supposed to. Not that everything is perfect. But that constant feeling of danger is gone."

"That's good," the doctor says with a wide grin.

***

Now he wants to explore the messages I believe about myself and how they originated.

"Having parents who were abusive and didn't take time to listen has had an adverse effect on your self esteem. Your parents gave you the message that you didn't matter, you were an annoyance, and needed to just shut up and go away. It's good to remember where those messages are coming from. They're from your past. They're not relevant any longer."

"I always feel like my words annoy people, especially you," I confess. "Are you *sure* it's okay for me to talk?" I'll ask that question again and again in our sessions, already knowing the answer but needing to quiet the missives of yesteryear.

Wittingly or unwittingly, Brock reinforced my parents' messages. His terse behavior felt familiar and the messages he communicated were much like the messages of my childhood. No wonder my emotions reverted to those of a needy kid.

"You have difficulty trusting people and trusting yourself." This, from the usually lenient doctor, induces yet another internal skirmish. *Is he accusing me? Is he just using far fewer words to echo what I've already stated? Mirroring, I think it's called.*

***

"I suck at relationships. I'm a serial saboteur," I tell him. "The more I screw up, the less willing I am to try again. It's like a cumulative wound. Trust means making myself vulnerable and there is very little that merits vulnerability anymore." And I stop myself before adding *except coming here where I'm placing enormous reliance on your ethical code of conduct.*

As if reading my mind, the doctor tells me he's aware of my inability to trust and is careful not to repeat any of my parents' or Brock's pathology.

I suppose there is an element of risk for him, too. He knows about my history of volatility. Maybe he's worried that I won't be willing to put the brakes on my impetuosity. Maybe I'll stalk him or lash out like I did with Brock. If he *is* worried, his professionally-induced poker face hides it.

"I guess I'm just more careful now with what I believe about people because I don't want to *ever* be put in the position I was with Brock."

"I don't think you ever will," the doctor says, smiling. He's more confident in me than I am.

***

I'm coming to terms with my laundry list of disorders. The doctor shows me the results of the *Minnesota Multiphasic Personality Inventory-2 Questionnaire*. Oddly, the "disorder" diagnoses, although a tad scary, are infinitely more comforting than my habitual denigrating self-diagnosis of "demon possessed, crazy total loser."

The inside me is officially out. I've got a file. It expands dramatically when the hospital relinquishes the notes from my psych ward stint in 1993. The discharge summary report states, among other things, "Diagnosis: Axis I: Major depression, panic disorder. Axis II: Likely, borderline personality disorder." Well, yes. Since then I've done research and discovered that during my worst times, I presented all nine *DSM-IV-TR* criterions for BPD.

As I describe to the doctor the goings on during that time, he states with confidence, "classic postpartum depression," a diagnosis mysteriously missing from the hospital's notes. But it was 1993, before Andrea Yates made headlines with her egregious child drownings under the influence of postpartum psychosis. Doctors rarely screened for emotional problems. Even if my doctor did ask, I probably dismissed it as an informal inquiry, not an actual screening for a diagnosis.

Freed from Brock's ban on self-help books, I get my hands on a copy of *Down Came the Rain* and then *Postpartum Depression for Dummies*. The words are clear. Women with a history of anxiety and "dysthymic" disorders, which is the technical term for depression, are at higher risk for developing postpartum depression. And the symptoms can be more extreme with each succeeding pregnancy. The pages reveal that those blood-letting images were about my mind keeping overly attentive to exaggerated dangers my children could face at any moment. My mind was inventing worst case scenarios so that I could prevent them from actually happening.

"It didn't feel like that, though. It felt like I *wanted* to hurt my kids."

Reconciling psychological and physiological explanations with demonic assumptions takes some doing. There remains an infinitesimal part of my gray matter that adheres itself to Brock and his doctrines, even knowing that I had been so extremely duped, brainwashed, gaslighted.

"You were *impaired*," the doctor says and I'm aware of a cathartic shred of dignity.

"Thank you for saying that, doctor. Maybe I should stop blaming myself."

***

My mind wanders back to 1978 and those drives Steve and I took to visit our first church. I was seventeen; Steve was twenty-one. We were both young and impressionable, searching for the meaning of life. Oh, how I labored over the words of that pastor. He seemed so emphatic and self-assured, proclaiming that bad thoughts were demonic and that I needed to rebuke them and pray. Despite devoting my entire adult life to praying and rebuking, I'd been powerless and then exhausted and discouraged. Learning that my problems aren't spiritual but organic in nature, likely stemming from a traumatic birth and childhood with a biological proclivity takes all the air out of the pastor's balloon and leaves me with a pile of deflated bullshit. There is such relief in not feeling so hopelessly inadequate and like a second class Christian.

***

"Brock would throw the *healed* term around like a buzz word on Ritalin. Yet the concept was so nebulous to me. When I'd ask him, he could never really give me a straight answer. So, I'll ask you, doctor, what is healed? What does it look like? How do I know when I'm healed?"

"Among other things, being healed is being able to function in today's world while simultaneously dealing with past issues."

Okay. Hmm. No magic panacea. No dramatic transformation. It's just a matter of being able to balance life.

"No magic bullet?" I joke.

"No, not really. Getting the patient stabilized and functioning is always top priority. Once that has occurred, we can explore past issues. I suspect that seems backwards from the unconventional help of your past."

"Totally. Brock would run these elusive experiments. If I got hysterical, he'd believe he was close to a breakthrough. His premise was that demons were manipulating my emotions, and a demonstrative demon seemed to ignite a certain kind of thrill in him. Brock was convinced that my birth family was evil and that they were all members of some world-domination conspiracy like the Illuminati. Sometimes I wonder if you're part of that same conspiracy, doctor," I confess.

"What do you mean?"

"Well, there is this tiny part of me that still holds on to Brock's beliefs. One of those beliefs is that everyone of influence is part of the Illuminati."

"Really? Including me?"

"Yeah. So are you? Not that you'd tell me even if you were."

"No, I'm not," he says, knowing that his answer isn't going to be good enough to satisfy me.

I tell him how I remember running around the gravel driveway loop, my body trying to outrun my mind, trying to separate or unite the two, I'm not sure which. Under Brock's influence, I concluded that none of the thoughts I held were my own. Every daydream, every impulse, every concept, idea, opinion, *everything, my entire mind* was demonic. I couldn't trust anything I thought or felt because it was all demonic. This was the worst effect Brock's influence had on me, that I lost my capacity to believe myself, my own thought processes. There was no me. I was a demon. Trying to outrun myself. Pure hell.

***

Then there's the validity of what I was actually "remembering" while ensnared in the visions and nightmares.

"Is it possible for a person to conjure up memories? Is the mind capable of making something seem like it actually happened? Make it seem real when it wasn't?" I need to know from a professional standpoint whether I was capable of this, because if I was capable, I was probably culpable. I've asked the doctor this question numerous times over what is now spanning several years, but he always answers me patiently.

"Yes," the doctor says, "especially since you were under so much duress from the postpartum issues while under the influence of Brock." He reiterates that my pseudo-memories come from the precipitating factors: anxiety disorder, postpartum psychosis, an abusive childhood, and an unwavering need to please. I was ripe for misguidance. It was the perfect storm.

I've done a lot of reading on the subject of women from the '90s who sought counseling from unscrupulous therapists who believed in the prevalence of satanic cults. These women described the same things: resurfaced "memories" and over-dependence on the counselor they were supposed to trust.

***

The more perplexing, and still unresolved, issues are my sleep disorders and the things I saw during those horrific episodes. There were the "flashbacks" where seemingly familiar yet foreign events came with a full spectrum of emotions. I still, to this day, have episodes, but they don't hold as much power.

There is also the sleep paralysis with its vivid, evil, sometimes sexual component. On rare occasion I'll have a mild episode. I'd like more information on these issues but my research hasn't afforded much.

***

Eventually, with the passage of time and the doctor's unwavering help—do I detect a subtle righteous indignation in him?—I am able to admit fully to Brock's egregious diagnosis and treatment plan and that I made a terrible mistake in devoting myself to his procedures. My hesitation has been caused by pride. Having to eat crow and admit how wrong I was is not an easy task.

Brock believed my symptoms were spiritual and that I was the victim of a cult, yet his personality and methods for helping me were very cult-like. With his disregard for appropriate boundaries and professional protocols, his influence made me wary of outsiders and gave me a sense of superiority about being "chosen." I felt a need to be secretive as well as an inordinate dependence on my leader. My world view was colored by fear and paranoia.

I have to bring into question my prayer for confirmation, the sign I believed was my go-ahead signal straight from the heavens. I don't have any explanation for it except that maybe God really did want me to endure all of that. Maybe there is a reason that has yet to reveal itself.

Healing can only occur when I'm honest with myself. I can't play the victim role any longer or blame all of my misfortunes on Brock, Steve, my parents, or any unseen enemies. I have to rely on psychology for insights into my erroneous behaviors and misconceptions, then change them into healthy ones.

***

"Have you thought about reconnecting with your siblings? I can understand your hesitance with your parents, but your siblings suffered just like you and would probably be a source of encouragement."

After letting the doctor's suggestion sufficiently percolate, I contact Sarah. It's been fifteen years and I'm worried that she'll be angry with me. But she's not. Instead she displays a genuine, undeserving love that reunites us as sisters. A few months later, Nellie has the same response. Things are still distant between Adam and me, but my hope is that maybe this part of the story has a happy ending, too.

***

Finally, the need to know my history takes a backseat to *living*. The mystery of whether my Masonic grandfather was one of *them* remains veiled and intangible but I'm okay with not knowing for sure whether I was ritually abused or not. The same is true for my waning sleep disorder. The need to know why is not a high priority any longer. Perhaps at some future date it will all make sense.

Life goes on and the therapy comes to an end. With a goodbye hug, I leave the doctor's office for the last time. And waiting for me are the best years of my life.

Freud wrote, "Love and work are the cornerstones of our humanness." I now feel human.

I've got a lot of lost time to make up for.

About the Author

Grace Peterson divides her time between working as an administrative assistant, writing and gardening. She is a member of The Association of Writing Excellence and The National Association of Memoir Writers and has published essays in several anthologies. She authors two blogs and writes a newspaper garden column. She is the proud mother of four grown children, four friendly felines, and has been married to her best friend since 1980. Her second book is in publication. Please visit her blog at www.gracepete.com.

ALL THINGS THAT MATTER PRESS, INC.

FOR MORE INFORMATION ON TITLES AVAILABLE FROM
ALL THINGS THAT MATTER PRESS, GO TO
http://allthingsthatmatterpress.com
or contact us at
allthingsthatmatterpress@gmail.com

www.ingramcontent.com/pod-product-compliance
Lightning Source LLC
Chambersburg PA
CBHW071432090426
42737CB00011B/1641